Network Security with pfSense

Architect, deploy, and operate enterprise-grade firewalls

Manuj Aggarwal

BIRMINGHAM - MUMBAI

Network Security with pfSense

Commissioning Editor: Vijin Boricha
Acquisition Editor: Prachi Bisht
Content Development Editor: Deepti Thore
Technical Editor: Nirbhaya Shaji
Copy Editor: Safis Editing
Project Coordinator: Kinjal Bari
Proofreader: Safis Editing
Indexer: Mariammal Chettiyar
Graphics: Jisha Chirayil
Production Coordinator: Deepika Naik

First published: July 2018

Production reference: 1280718

Published by Packt Publishing Ltd.
Livery Place
35 Livery Street
Birmingham
B3 2PB, UK.

ISBN 978-1-78953-297-5

www.packtpub.com

`mapt.io`

Mapt is an online digital library that gives you full access to over 5,000 books and videos, as well as industry leading tools to help you plan your personal development and advance your career. For more information, please visit our website.

Why subscribe?

- Spend less time learning and more time coding with practical eBooks and Videos from over 4,000 industry professionals

- Improve your learning with Skill Plans built especially for you

- Get a free eBook or video every month

- Mapt is fully searchable

- Copy and paste, print, and bookmark content

PacktPub.com

Did you know that Packt offers eBook versions of every book published, with PDF and ePub files available? You can upgrade to the eBook version at `www.PacktPub.com` and as a print book customer, you are entitled to a discount on the eBook copy. Get in touch with us at `service@packtpub.com` for more details.

At `www.PacktPub.com`, you can also read a collection of free technical articles, sign up for a range of free newsletters, and receive exclusive discounts and offers on Packt books and eBooks.

Contributor

About the author

Manuj Aggarwal is an entrepreneur, investor, and a technology enthusiast. He likes startups, business ideas, and high-tech anything. He loves to work on hard problems and get his hands dirty with cutting-edge technologies. Currently, he is the principal consultant, architect, and CTO of a software consulting company, TetraNoodle Technologies, based in Vancouver, Canada. He is passionate about sharing all the knowledge that he has acquired over the years.

Packt is searching for authors like you

If you're interested in becoming an author for Packt, please visit `authors.packtpub.com` and apply today. We have worked with thousands of developers and tech professionals, just like you, to help them share their insight with the global tech community. You can make a general application, apply for a specific hot topic that we are recruiting an author for, or submit your own idea.

Table of Contents

Preface   1

Chapter 1: Introduction to pfSense   5
  What is pfSense?   6
  Benefits of pfSense   8
  Use cases   8
    LAN or WAN router   9
    Wireless hotspot or captive portal   9
    VPN router   9
    Firewall   9
    DHCP or DNS server   10
    Multi-WAN router support for failover or load balancer   10
    Port forwarding or Network Address Translation   10
  pfSense features   11
  Prerequisites for installation   12
  Installing pfSense on a virtual machine   15
  Launching the virtual machine   18
  Configuring VM and completing the installation   19
  Configuring pfSense   25
  pfSense WebGUI walkthrough   36
  Configuring pfSense as a DHCP server   45
  Summary   56

Chapter 2: pfSense as a Firewall   57
  What is a firewall?   57
  Configuring pfSense as a firewall   60
  Setting up firewall rules   65
    Firewall rules in pfSense   72
      Firewall rules for internal LAN networks   76
        Setting up firewall rules for LAN2   78
  Managing firewall rules   81
  Summary   82

Chapter 3: pfSense as a Failover and Load Balancer   83
  Load balancing and failover   83
  Load balancing and failover across multiple WAN connections   88
  Configuring Gateway Groups   90
  Verifying load balancing across WAN connections   96
  Failover across multiple WAN connections   97
  Summary   99

Chapter 4: Remote Connectivity with pfSense and IPsec   101
  What is IPsec?   101
    Transport mode   102
    Tunnel mode   102
    IPsec features   103
  Security Association   103
  IPsec VPN tunnel implementation   104
  Prerequisites   105
  IPsec phases   105
  Configuring IPsec tunnel   105
  Configuring pfSense firewall rules   113
  Summary   117

Chapter 5: Using pfSense as a Squid Proxy Server   119
  The proxy server   120
    The Squid proxy server   121
  Installing the Squid proxy server   123
  Configuring the Squid proxy server   124
  Testing the Squid proxy server   134
  Summary   137

Other Books You May Enjoy   139

Index   143

Preface

According to a recent study conducted by a major cyber-security firm, only less than half the online population understands the term firewalls, or even knows if they have one enabled on their PC. Firewalls are much more important in a corporate or work environment. They not only keep the corporate network safe, but can also optimize traffic routing and provide a whole range of other benefits. If you're connected to the internet, you are a potential target of an array of cyber threats, such as hackers, keyloggers, and Trojans that attack through unpatched security holes. This means that if you, like most people, shop and bank online, then you are vulnerable to identity theft and other malicious attacks. A firewall works as a barrier or a shield between your PC and cyberspace. When you're connected to the internet, you're continually sending and receiving information in small units called packets. The firewall filters these packets to see whether they meet certain criteria set by a series of rules. And after that, it blocks or allows the data. This way, hackers cannot get inside and steal information, such as bank account numbers and passwords from you.

Basic firewalls, such as the one included in your operating systems, only monitor incoming traffic by default. This may give you a false sense of security. Keep in mind that outgoing traffic with your credit card information, bank accounts, and social security number is not protected. A good firewall will monitor traffic in both directions, that is both your incoming data and your outgoing data, keeping your private information safe. In addition to preventing unauthorized access to your PC, it also makes your PC invisible when you're online, helping prevent attempted intrusions in the first place. Firewalls are one of the most critical parts of a network. It's the first line of defense that your system has against attacks or unwanted visitors. And it makes all the difference in ensuring that your data is protected. pfSense is a highly versatile, open source routing and firewall software. With thousands of enterprises using pfSense software, it is quickly becoming the world's most trusted open source network security solution. pfSense has all of the features you would find in a commercial firewall solution and more. And it is absolutely free. And better yet, you can customize pfSense based on your organization's requirements and create a unique solution that is perfect for you. In this book, you'll learn about pfSense, all of its key features, how you can install and deploy it, as well as the different tasks you can perform.

Who this book is for

This book is for IT administrators, security administrators, anyone running a home or small office network, technical architects, founders, and CXOs.

What this book covers

Chapter 1, *Introduction to pfSense*, helps you gain an understanding of what pfSense is, what its key features are, and its advantages.

Chapter 2, *pfSense as a Firewall*, explains how to configure pfSense as a firewall, and create and manage firewall rules.

Chapter 3, *pfSense as a Failover and Load Balancer*, covers how to configure and test pfSense for failover and load balancing across multiple WAN connections.

Chapter 4, *Remote Connectivity with pfSense and IPSec*, explains how you can implement IPsec tunnels with pfSense. You will learn about its features, and how it is configured and used.

Chapter 5, *Using pfSense as a Squid Proxy Server*, covers how to configure and integrate pfSense as a Squid proxy server.

To get the most out of this book

In this book, we have used the latest stable version of pfSense, which is 2.4.3. The minimum hardware requirements, as of the latest version, are 500 Mhz CPU and 512 MB of RAM. The recommended requirements are a bit higher than these such as 1 Ghz CPU and 1 GB of RAM.

For some of the topics, you may need to take some initial steps, such as signing up for services and launching a virtual machine.

Download the color images

We also provide a PDF file that has color images of the screenshots/diagrams used in this book. You can download it here: https://www.packtpub.com/sites/default/files/downloads/NetworkSecuritywithpfSense_ColorImages.pdf.

Conventions used

There are a number of text conventions used throughout this book.

`CodeInText`: Indicates code words in text, database table names, folder names, filenames, file extensions, pathnames, dummy URLs, user input, and Twitter handles. Here is an example: "Enter the desired **Name** of the VM, select `BSD` from the **Type** drop-down menu, and select `FreeBSD (64-bit)` from the **Version** drop-down menu."

Any command-line input or output is written as follows:

```
ping 192.168.1.1 -t
```

Bold: Indicates a new term, an important word, or words that you see onscreen. For example, words in menus or dialog boxes appear in the text like this. Here is an example: "In this scenario, pfSense acts as a **DHCP Server**, **Firewall**, and **NAT** device. It can play these roles distinctly or all at the same time simultaneously."

Warnings or important notes appear like this.

Tips and tricks appear like this.

Get in touch

Feedback from our readers is always welcome.

General feedback: Email `feedback@packtpub.com` and mention the book title in the subject of your message. If you have questions about any aspect of this book, please email us at `questions@packtpub.com`.

Errata: Although we have taken every care to ensure the accuracy of our content, mistakes do happen. If you have found a mistake in this book, we would be grateful if you would report this to us. Please visit www.packtpub.com/submit-errata, selecting your book, clicking on the Errata Submission Form link, and entering the details.

Piracy: If you come across any illegal copies of our works in any form on the Internet, we would be grateful if you would provide us with the location address or website name. Please contact us at copyright@packtpub.com with a link to the material.

If you are interested in becoming an author: If there is a topic that you have expertise in and you are interested in either writing or contributing to a book, please visit authors.packtpub.com.

Reviews

Please leave a review. Once you have read and used this book, why not leave a review on the site that you purchased it from? Potential readers can then see and use your unbiased opinion to make purchase decisions, we at Packt can understand what you think about our products, and our authors can see your feedback on their book. Thank you!

For more information about Packt, please visit packtpub.com.

Introduction to pfSense
1

his book aims to provide you with in-depth knowledge of a very widely used technology, **pfSense**. This will provide you with some real-world scenarios and use cases, which you will be able to leverage immediately in your own projects. The introductory modules will help you to understand what pfSense is, its features, the key services it provides, and how you can install it. After the introductory modules, we will deep dive into each of its exciting features. You'll learn about the installation, configuration, and use of pfSense. This education will enable you to do everything from setting up firewalls, load balancing, and failover settings, to integrating with other software such as **OpenVPN** and **Squid** proxy server.

In this book, we will give you the information you need in order to work with this amazing piece of software.

In this chapter, you will be introduced to pfSense. You will gain an understanding of what pfSense is, its key features, and its advantages. You will also view demonstrations on the installation of pfSense on a virtual platform on VMware, as well as some other configurations. Let's get started.

What is pfSense?

pfSense is a free, customized distribution of **FreeBSD**. FreeBSD itself is an operating system for a variety of platforms, which focuses on features, speed, and stability. It's derived from BSD, the version of UNIX developed at the University of California, Berkeley. It is developed and maintained by a large community. You can use pfSense to turn a computer into a fully-featured router and firewall. This software was first developed in 2004 as an offshoot of the popular **m0n0wall** project. The main difference between pfSense and m0n0wall is that pfSense is designed for personal computers and servers instead of embedded devices. This allows pfSense to offer more flexibility and features. pfSense is a very flexible and powerful tool that you can easily adapt to numerous applications, from a home router to a firewall, for a large corporate network. pfSense is easy to install and maintain. It has a very useful web-based user interface. pfSense also has many features that are usually only found in expensive commercial routers. You can use the following three types of install media to install pfSense:

1. **Optical disk image**: That could be an ISO image, a CD, or a DVD disc. This is an easy and familiar choice. Use this option if the target hardware has an optical drive. This is especially useful if the BIOS will not boot from USB.
2. **Memstick:** This option is similar to the CD or DVD, but runs the installation from a USB thumb drive. It's often faster than a CD or DVD. This is very useful with new devices, as many of them don't have integrated optical drives, making this the current best recommendation.
3. **Serial memstick**: This option is similar to the memstick image, but runs using the serial console rather than VGA for newer embedded systems.

The following is the graphical representation of the installation media:

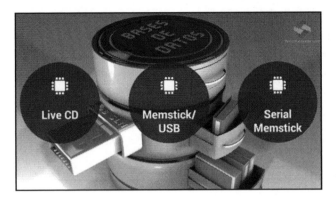

pfSense is a very impressive software. The following are some of its key features:

- pfSense is very robust and it supports a number of great features. This allows you to have a single device that performs all the functions you need at the edge of your network. The downside of this is that all your functions work from a single machine, so it's a single point of failure.
- To offset this, pfSense also supports high availability, which means that you can group several devices together.
- One of the most significant benefits is that pfSense is free. You can simply download the software from the website. Although virtualization is supported, you will, of course, need to spend on the hardware that you are going to install the software on. However, all things considered, it is more cost-effective than other solutions.
- pfSense can be installed on any hardware, which makes it highly flexible and very scalable.
- pfSense is also highly extensible. It has an energetic and dedicated community behind it. They have built and contributed tons of useful add-ons to the pfSense platform. Most of these add-ons are also completely free.

Benefits of pfSense

The first benefit is that pfSense is feature-rich, robust, and very flexible software. Besides the essential firewall features, it has tons of additional features for network routing, remote connectivity, diagnostics, and reporting, along with many more. What's more, it is an extensible platform. You do not have to settle for the functionality provided out of the box with pfSense. You're free to write your own plugins and add-ons. Many members of the community have done just that. You will go over some of its key extensions later in this book.

With all the enterprise-grade features and security pfSense provides, it is incredible that it is a free and open source product. This is possibly its biggest benefit. You can download it from the pfSense website at `https://www.pfsense.org/download/`, and install it by yourself. For large implementations and complex configurations, you do have the option to purchase license support from professionals, but that is completely optional.

pfSense is very versatile and flexible. If you are a professional working out of a home-based office, you can use pfSense to protect your network. But if you are a large company running a global infrastructure, you can still use pfSense to protect various parts of your work. pfSense can run on a 10-year-old PC with limited resources, and it can also run on large multicore servers. This makes it quite scalable. You can easily expand the resources on your pfSense infrastructure in the event that your network needs an increase. And due to these benefits, and many other features which pfSense brings to the table, individuals, network administrators, security enthusiasts, and companies across the world are embracing pfSense. These are just some of the most recognizable names who have adopted pfSense as a core part of their network infrastructure. Needless to say, with organizations such as Google, the US Department of Homeland Security, Shopify, and NASA putting their faith in pfSense, this free open source firewall solution is here to stay.

Use cases

Let's take a look at some use cases where pfSense can prove to be instrumental.

LAN or WAN router

pfSense can act as a LAN or WAN router. LAN, as you know, is basically a group of computers and associated devices that share a common communication line or wireless link to a server. A LAN usually consists of devices connected within a closed area, such as an office or a commercial establishment. A WAN is a geographically distributed private telecommunications network that interconnects multiple LANs. For example, in an organization, a WAN might connect multiple branch offices. A router is used to connect a LAN to a WAN.

Wireless hotspot or captive portal

pfSense can work as a wireless hotspot. The pfSense appliance has significantly more functionality and configurability than a typical SOHO security appliance. It is also slightly more involved to set up. pfSense offers some great features, such as being able to host a Wi-Fi network for guests outside of the main firewall, even using a different public IP to NAT behind.

VPN router

You can also configure pfSense as a VPN router. A VPN is used to add security and privacy to private and public networks, such as Wi-Fi hotspots and the internet. VPNs are most often used by corporations to protect sensitive data.

Firewall

You can configure pfSense as a firewall to put rules and other security settings over the private network. A firewall is a network security system that uses rules to control incoming and outgoing network traffic. It acts as a barrier between a trusted and untrusted network. A firewall controls access to the resources of a network through a positive control model. This means that the only traffic allowed onto the network is defined in the firewall policy. All other traffic is denied.

DHCP or DNS server

pfSense can act as a DNS server or DHCP server. DHCP is a communications protocol that network administrators use to centrally manage and automate the network configuration of devices attaching to an IP network. It removes the need to manually configure IP addresses and automatically assigns an IP address to a device, even when moving to different locations. DHCP is supported for both IPv4 and IPv6, that is, the Internet Protocol version. With the use of DHCP and domain name resolution all on the firewall, it makes life easier for configuring the network traffic precisely the way you need it.

Multi-WAN router support for failover or load balancer

This support for multiple WAN connections enables pfSense to load balance or failover traffic from a LAN to multiple internet connections. With load balancing, traffic from the LAN is shared out on a connection-based, round-robin basis across the available WANs. With failover, traffic will go out to the highest-priority WAN, until it goes down. Then, the next one is used. pfSense monitors each WAN connection using either the gateway IP or an alternate monitor IP address, and if the monitor fails, it will remove that WAN from use. This also reduces latency to users. Load balancing can be implemented with hardware, software, or a combination of both.

Port forwarding or Network Address Translation

You can also use pfSense to forward ports or **Network Address Translation** (**NAT**). NAT is the process where a network device, usually a firewall, assigns a public address to a computer or group of computers inside a private network. The main use of NAT is to limit the number of public IP addresses an organization or company must use for both economy and security purposes. NAT helps improve security and decrease the number of IP addresses an organization needs. NAT gateways sit between the two networks—the inside network and the outside network. Systems on the inside network are typically assigned IP addresses that cannot be routed to external networks.

pfSense features

Let's discuss the pfSense features through a use-case diagram:

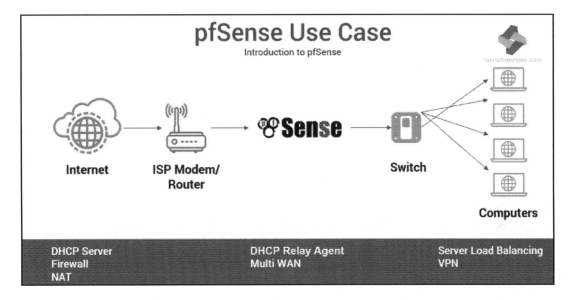

The preceding diagram gives you an idea of how pfSense plays a vital role in the network. The **ISP Modem/Router** connects pfSense to the internet. The **Switch** connects pfSense to various desktops.

In this scenario, pfSense acts as a **DHCP Server**, **Firewall**, and **NAT** device. It can play these roles distinctly or all at the same time simultaneously.

Let's explore some other standard features of pfSense:

- The **DHCP Relay Agent** feature serves the DHCP service for all clients.
- The **Firewall** feature filters requests and responses by source and destination IPs, and source and destination ports. It also limits simultaneous connections on a per rules basis.
- **NAT** port forwards include range and use of multiple public IPs and one-to-one **NAT** for individual IP or multiple subnets.
- The **Multi WAN** functionality enables the use of multiple internet connections, with load balancing, failover, and usage distribution. With this, you can achieve redundancy across multiple ISP connections, and not only that, you can distribute the traffic from your internal network to the internet to numerous links in a load-balanced fashion.

As a VPN server, pfSense offers two options for VPN connectivity:

- IPsec allows connectivity with any device supporting standard IPsec. This is most commonly used for site-to-site connectivity to other pfSense installations, and almost all other firewall solutions like Cisco, Juniper, and so on. It can also be used for mobile client connectivity.
- The second is OpenVPN. OpenVPN is a flexible, powerful SSL VPN solution supporting a wide range of client operating systems. Let's assume that the computers are in different sites. You can use IPsec VPN to connect them both together.

Now that you're familiar with pfSense, let's go ahead with installation and configuration of pfSense. But before we start with that, let's review the minimum hardware requirements for installing and running pfSense.

Prerequisites for installation

For some of the topics in this book, you may need to take some more initial steps, such as signing up for services and launching a virtual machine.

In this book, we have used the latest stable version of pfSense, which is 2.4.3. pfSense is an open source software and occasionally releases new versions or patches. So, in order to review the latest requirements, you should always refer to the latest documentation. So, let's review it now.

Navigate to the pfSense site's requirements page at `https://www.pfsense.org/products/`. This page lists some ready-made appliances, which are tried and tested by the pfSense community. If you want to avoid the hassle of building your server and trying out all the components, then it is recommended that you purchase one of the appliances. But, of course, if you are like a tinkerer or a geek, then you can opt for the option of building your server.

Let's review the hardware requirements for building your own server:

pfSense Hardware Requirements and Guidance

The following outlines the minimum hardware requirements for pfSense 2.x. Note the minimum requirements are not suitable for all environments. You may be able to get by with less than the minimum, but with less memory you may start swapping to disk, which will dramatically slow down your system.

General Requirements:

Minimum	• CPU - 500 Mhz • RAM - 512 MB
Recommended	• CPU - 1 Ghz • RAM - 1 GB

Requirements Specific to Individual Platforms:

Full Install	• CD-ROM or USB for initial installation • 1 GB hard drive

As you can see, the minimum requirements, as of the latest version, are very modest. pfSense can run on a PC with **500 Mhz CPU** and **512 MB** of **RAM**. Do you know of any sophisticated software that is capable of running on these low specs? Anyway, the recommended requirements are a bit higher than these. But still, **1 Ghz CPU** and **1 GB** of **RAM** is still very modest by modern standards. Here are some additional details for specific components of the system. You can check the compatibility of your network interface cards here as well:

Hardware Compatibility List

As pfSense is based on FreeBSD, its hardware compatibility list is the same as FreeBSD's. The pfSense kernel includes all FreeBSD drivers.

> **PFSENSE 2.4 (FREEBSD 11.1)**

This is very important because pfSense is a firewall and its primary function is securing your network. Besides that, there is also a link to the compatibility list for FreeBSD:

FreeBSD 11.1-RELEASE Hardware Notes

The FreeBSD Documentation Project

Copyright © 2000-2017 The FreeBSD Documentation Project

FreeBSD is a registered trademark of the FreeBSD Foundation.

AMD, AMD Athlon, AMD Opteron, AMD Phenom, AMD Sempron, AMD Turion, Athlon, Élan, Opteron, and PCnet are trademarks of Advanced Micro Devices, Inc.

Fujitsu, the Fujitsu logo, LifeBook, Stylistic, PRIMEPOWER, PRIMEQUEST, PRIMECLUSTER, ETERNUS, TRIOLE, ESPRIMO, BioMedCACHe, CACHe, CELLINJECTOR, isS, Materials Explorer, SystemWalker, and Interstage are trademarks or registered trademarks of Fujitsu Limited in the United States and other countries.

IBM, AIX, OS/2, PowerPC, PS/2, S/390, and ThinkPad are trademarks of International Business Machines Corporation in the United States, other countries, or both.

Intel, Celeron, Centrino, Core, EtherExpress, i386, i486, Itanium, Pentium, and Xeon are trademarks or registered trademarks of Intel Corporation or its subsidiaries in the United States and other countries.

SPARC, SPARC64, and UltraSPARC are trademarks of SPARC International, Inc in the United States and other countries. SPARC International, Inc owns all of the SPARC trademarks and under licensing agreements allows the proper use of these trademarks by its members.

Sun, Sun Microsystems, Java, Java Virtual Machine, JDK, JRE, JSP, JVM, Netra, OpenJDK, Solaris, StarOffice, SunOS and VirtualBox are trademarks or registered trademarks of Sun Microsystems, Inc. in the United States and other countries.

Many of the designations used by manufacturers and sellers to distinguish their products are claimed as trademarks. Where those designations appear in this document, and the FreeBSD Project was aware of the trademark claim, the designations have been followed by the "™" or the "®" symbol.

Last modified on 2017-06-29 19:38:21 EDT by gjb.

Table of Contents
1. Introduction
2. Supported Processors and System Boards
    2.1. amd64
    2.2. i386
    2.3. pc98

As mentioned earlier, pfSense is based on FreeBSD. So, it'll make sense to check the compatibility of your hardware with the FreeBSD compatibility list as well.

Now that you know all about pfSense and its features, let's install pfSense on a virtual machine.

Installing pfSense on a virtual machine

First and foremost, you need to download the installer files for pfSense.

1. To download pfSense, navigate to `https://www.pfsense.org/download/`:

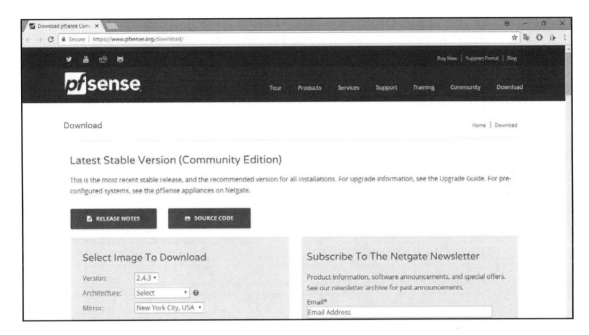

pfSense supports multiple platforms and flavors. It also has various editions and versions available. For the best results, always use the stable version. And, of course, unless you intend to purchase the supported version, opt for the free Community Edition. That is exactly what we'll do here as well.

2. From the **Version** drop-down list choose 2.4.3, which is the stable version we are using. The **Architecture** specifies the target CPU architecture you intend to use. Select the option depending on your computer. If your system has a 64-bit capable Intel or AMD CPU, use the 64-bit version. The 32-bit version should only be used with 32-bit CPUs. In this case, we will pick **AMD64(64-bit)**. pfSense also supports multiple types of **Installer** options:

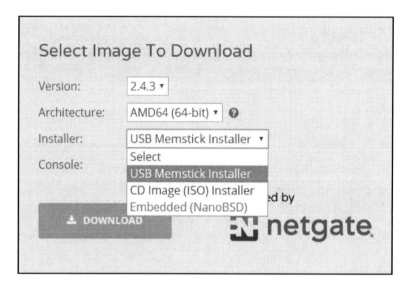

You can download the **Installer** as a **USB Memstick Installer**, ISO CD image, or as an **Embedded (NanoBSD)** image. The USB memory stick image is meant to be written to the hard disk of your target system. Installing pfSense on the hard drive is the preferred method of running pfSense software. In this case, the entire hard drive is overwritten. Note that dual booting with another OS is not supported. The **CD Image (ISO) Installer** is used to create a CD or DVD version that's used to install on virtual machines or systems with a CD or DVD drive. The Embedded version of pfSense is meant to be written to system hard disk before use, and it is specifically tailored for use with any hardware using flash memory, mostly compact flash, rather than the system's hard drive. As you may be aware, flash memory can only handle a limited number of writes, so the embedded version runs read-only from flash with read/write file systems as RAM disks. The NanoBSD platform has two **OS slices** and a **config slice**. One OS slice is used to boot from, the other is used for upgrades. The config slice is where the configuration resides. There are two variations of the NanoBSD platform, namely, the default version, which uses a serial console, and another that supports using a VGA console. Each of these variations also come sized for different sizes of storage media. For this instance, in the **Installer** drop-down list, select **CD Image (ISO) Installer**.

3. In the **Mirror** dropdown, select the nearest location to you, and then click on the **DOWNLOAD** button. Mirror sites are useful when the original site generates too much traffic for a single server to support. Mirror sites also increase the speed with which files or websites can be accessed. Users can download files more quickly from a server that is geographically closer to them.

4. After selecting these options, let's click on the **DOWNLOAD** button to get the required installer files. After the download is complete, once you go to the download folder, you will be able to locate the pfSense installer file. As you will see, the installer file is in a zipped compressed format. You can unarchive this file using any usual compression utility such as WinZip, or WinRAR on Windows, and other similar programs on other platforms.

5. Once the ISO file has been extracted, you can burn the ISO to a CD, which will be a bootable CD, and use it to then install the software on your PC, that is, if you are using a physical hardware device. Alternatively, you can use the ISO file to create a virtual machine. You can also run pfSense in live CD mode, where you can just run the pfSense software from the CD without installing anything on your system's hard drive. The benefit here is that you can test drive pfSense without changing any configuration on your system. However the drawback is that you will lose all your configuration once your system restarts. So, for now, we will stick with permanent installation of pfSense on a virtual machine.

Let's go ahead and launch a new virtual machine for pfSense.

Launching the virtual machine

We will use VirtualBox for hosting the virtual machine, but you are free to use any other virtualization platform, such as VMware Workstation and Hyper-V:

1. After launching VirtualBox, we have to create a new virtual machine for pfSense by clicking on the **Machines** menu and then **New**:

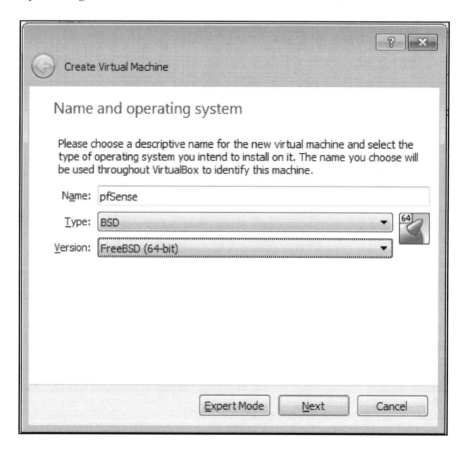

2. The **Create Virtual Machine** wizard will launch, which will walk you through the process of creating and launching a new virtual machine. The creation is rather straightforward, with default choices.

3. Enter the desired **Name** of the VM, select **BSD** from the **Type** drop-down menu, and select **FreeBSD(64-bit)** from the **Version** drop-down menu.

4. Select the desired RAM for your VM. The recommended size is 512 MB but it will run smoothly at 256 MB if you are running low on RAM.

5. Also further into the steps you can select the size of the virtual hard disk. We recommend at least 4 GB in size but the minimum requirement is 1 GB if you are running low on disk space. The click **Create**.

This will successfully create a virtual machine for you. Now, we are left with configuring and completing the installation.

Configuring VM and completing the installation

The VM is now created, but you still have some network configuration to do. pfSense is all about networking and security. And, so far, you have not allocated any network interface cards to this virtual machine. So, let's go ahead and proceed with the network configuration. After that, you need to finish the installation for pfSense.

Typically, pfSense isolates the network traffic for internal and external networks using different network interface cards. Consider a scenario where you have one network device that is connected directly to the internet, and the second network device is connected to the internal network. That is precisely how most pfSense installations are configured.

1. From the **Settings** menu in VirtualBox, go to **Network** settings. Currently only one network adapter will be enabled, **Adapter 1**, which will be the WAN network.

2. Now, we will add one more internal network adapter by clicking on **Adapter 2** and enabling it by checking the **Enable Network Adapter** check box:

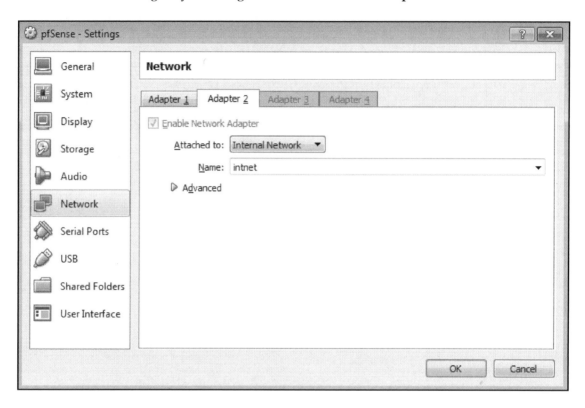

3. From the **Attached to** drop-down menu, select **Internal Network**. Within the context of VirtualBox, an **Internal Network** segment is a private network that is shared by other virtual machines. This LAN segment can be useful for multi-tier testing, network performance analysis, and situations where virtual machine isolation is important. After taking care of the internal network adapter, let's also mount the ISO image for pfSense software.

4. Go to the **Storage** settings from the **Settings** menu and select the **Live CD/DVD** check box.

5. Mount the pfSense ISO image to the CD-ROM by clicking on the **Optical Drive** drop-down menu:

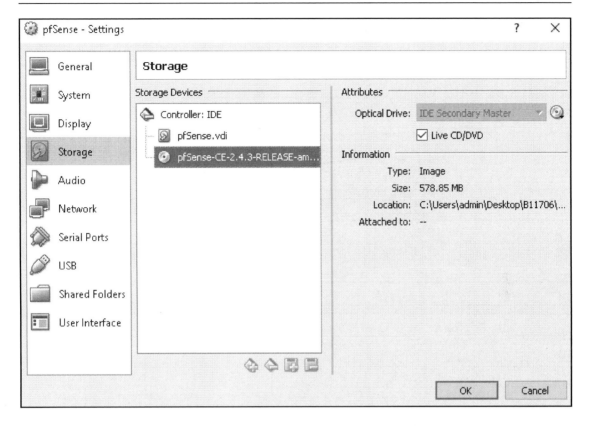

6. Click the **OK** button, which will save the settings. Now that the virtual machine has been configured properly, we can start the VM.

 Now, VirtualBox will launch this virtual machine. And since you have already mounted the bootable CD ISO image, it will boot into pfSense installer.

7. In the home screen of pfSense installer, you are given a few choices on how you want to install pfSense. The first and default option is **Boot Multi User**. This will continue the FreeBSD boot process. So, just proceed with the default options and press *Enter* to boot into the FreeBSD installer. The kernel will start to load and display the boot output. After a minute, a text prompt will appear to install or enter recovery mode.

8. Press *I* to launch the installer. The installer will start now and it will give us the opportunity to change the display and other system settings.

If no selection is made within 10 seconds, it will continue to the installer automatically.

9. Let's accept all the default settings:

```
┤ Select Task ├
Choose one of the following tasks to
perform.

< Quick/Easy Install >
< Custom Install >
< Rescue config.xml >
< Reboot >
< Exit >
```

Then, it offers the choice of a **Quick/Easy Install**, **Custom Install**, and several other options. Select **Quick/Easy Install** and press *Enter*. This easy install will take care of a lot of things such as disk partitions. Select **OK** and the installer will begin. pfSense will be installed on the first available disk in the system. It will take a few minutes to copy all of the files to the target disk, so allow it some time to finish. When the files have finished being copied, the installer will prompt to select either the **Embedded kernel** or **Standard Kernel**; select **Standard Kernel:**

```
┤ Install Kernel ├
You may now wish to install a custom Kernel configuration.

< Standard Kernel >
< Embedded kernel (no VGA console, keyboard >
```

Basically, this setting controls whether you get a VGA terminal or a serial-based console. If this were an embedded device with no video card, then we would have picked the **Embedded kernel** option. The installation continues.

10. Once the installation is complete, pfSense needs to reboot. So, press *Enter* to reboot. While rebooting, make sure you unmount the CD so that the virtual machine boots from its hard drive and not from the CD-ROM again.

11. Click on the **Remove Disk from Virtual Drive** from where we mounted the ISO image earlier. You can ignore any warning dialog which may pop up.

12. Now, let's get back to the virtual machine. The machine has rebooted, and this is the boot screen for pfSense:

13. Let's press *F1* to continue booting pfSense. Note that this time, it is booting from pfSense, which has been installed on the hard drive of this system. Once the installation part is complete, we will get a screen like the following:

```
Starting syslog...done.
Starting CRON... done.
pfSense 2.4.3-RELEASE amd64 Mon Mar 26 18:02:04 CDT 2018
Bootup complete

FreeBSD/amd64 (pfSense.localdomain) (ttyv0)

VirtualBox Virtual Machine - Netgate Device ID: 144f98f74a3a1848552f

*** Welcome to pfSense 2.4.3-RELEASE (amd64) on pfSense ***

 WAN (wan)         -> em0         -> v4/DHCP4: 10.0.2.15/24
 LAN (lan)         -> em1         -> v4: 192.168.1.1/24

 0) Logout (SSH only)                 9) pfTop
 1) Assign Interfaces                10) Filter Logs
 2) Set interface(s) IP address      11) Restart webConfigurator
 3) Reset webConfigurator password   12) PHP shell + pfSense tools
 4) Reset to factory defaults        13) Update from console
 5) Reboot system                    14) Enable Secure Shell (sshd)
 6) Halt system                      15) Restore recent configuration
 7) Ping host                        16) Restart PHP-FPM
 8) Shell

Enter an option: █
```

Here, you can see that one of the IP addresses and networking interfaces has been assigned to WAN's network connection. This is the em0 network interface. em1 has been assigned to the internal LAN network. The WAN network interface has been assigned a dynamic IP address. This is typical for general-purpose-based internet connections such as cable, ADSL, or fiber optic ISP connections. You may also be allocated a fixed IP from your ISP. These settings can easily be changed within the pfSense admin console, or right here on the admin console.

14. If you want to change the IP address, you can change it by selecting the second option: Set interface(s) IP address, to whatever you need to change it to. We will visit these shortly. The DHCP IP address assigned to the WAN connection is 10.0.2.15/24, while the LAN, or em1, has taken the network address 192.168.1.1/24. The LAN interface will become the internet gateway for all the devices within the internal LAN network.

Once the installation is complete, you need to configure pfSense. So, let's do that now.

Configuring pfSense

This next phase of configuration will be done through a web-based administration portal provided by pfSense. You can use this rich web interface to configure all your network components, firewall rules, VPN settings, and so on. The LAN network interface's IP address exposes this web-based administration console. So, in this case, you will navigate to the IP address 192.168.1.1 in order to access the administration portal for pfSense.

As the client machine, we have set up another virtual machine which is running Windows Server 2012 R2. Let's head over to the Windows Server.

Before we attempt to navigate to the pfSense web-based configuration portal from this client machine, let's make sure that this Windows Server virtual machine is on the same network as the pfSense server:

1. Let's access network settings for this Windows system. Right-click on the Windows **Home** icon and select **Network Connections**. This Windows machine only has one network adapter called **Ethernet0**.

2. Right-click on **Ethernet0** and select **Properties**. Now, double-click on **Internet Protocol Version 4 (TCP/IPv4)**. Change the IP address to 192.168.1.2, the gateway IP address to 192.168.1.1, and the DNS server to 192.168.1.1:

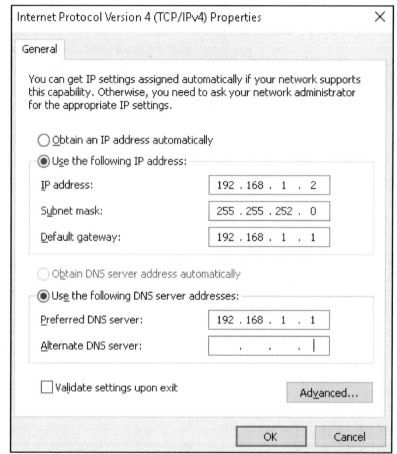

1.1.1.1
9.9.9.9

Here, we are trying to accomplish a few things with this configuration.

First, you need to make sure that the Windows client machine is on the same subnet as the pfSense server. Second, you want to make sure that this client machine is using pfSense as its default gateway and DNS server.

3. After configuring the IP settings, click on **OK**. Now, we can proceed with the next phase of configuration.
4. Right-click on the Windows Home icon and select **Run**. Run the cmd command to open the Command Prompt.
5. Let's try to ping the pfSense server. Execute the ping command as follows:

```
C:\Users\packt>ping 192.168.1.1 -t

Pinging 192.168.1.1 with 32 bytes of data:
Reply from 192.168.1.1: bytes=32 time<1ms TTL=64
Reply from 192.168.1.1: bytes=32 time<1ms TTL=64
Reply from 192.168.1.1: bytes=32 time<1ms TTL=64
Reply from 192.168.1.1: bytes=32 time<1ms TTL=64
Reply from 192.168.1.1: bytes=32 time<1ms TTL=64
Reply from 192.168.1.1: bytes=32 time<1ms TTL=64
Reply from 192.168.1.1: bytes=32 time<1ms TTL=64
Reply from 192.168.1.1: bytes=32 time<1ms TTL=64
Reply from 192.168.1.1: bytes=32 time<1ms TTL=64
Reply from 192.168.1.1: bytes=32 time<1ms TTL=64
Reply from 192.168.1.1: bytes=32 time<1ms TTL=64
Reply from 192.168.1.1: bytes=32 time<1ms TTL=64
Reply from 192.168.1.1: bytes=32 time<1ms TTL=64
Reply from 192.168.1.1: bytes=32 time<1ms TTL=64
Reply from 192.168.1.1: bytes=32 time<1ms TTL=64
Reply from 192.168.1.1: bytes=32 time<1ms TTL=64
Reply from 192.168.1.1: bytes=32 time<1ms TTL=64

Ping statistics for 192.168.1.1:
    Packets: Sent = 17, Received = 17, Lost = 0 (0% loss),
Approximate round trip times in milli-seconds:
    Minimum = 0ms, Maximum = 0ms, Average = 0ms
Control-C
^C
C:\Users\packt>
```

Here, `192.168.1.1` is the IP address of the pfSense server. The `-t` option pings the specified host until it is asked to stop. Since we're getting replies, it confirms that the connection is working absolutely fine.

6. Press *Ctrl + C* to stop the `ping` command.

7. Execute `exit` to close the command window.

Now that the connectivity has been established, it is time for us to get familiar with the configuration portal for pfSense.

8. Launch your favorite browser and navigate to the pfSense server's IP address `192.168.1.1`. By default, pfSense exposes the configuration portal over an HTTPS endpoint. It uses a self-signed SSL certificate for this purpose. Your browser may complain about the security certificate. You can safely ignore it and proceed. An SSL-enabled connection is more secure, even with this self-signed certificate, as long as you are familiar with the source of the certificate.

What we will be looking at once the page loads will be the login page for the pfSense server. The default username and password is `admin` and `pfsense`, respectively. Note that it is all in lowercase.

9. Enter the credentials and click on **SIGN IN**:

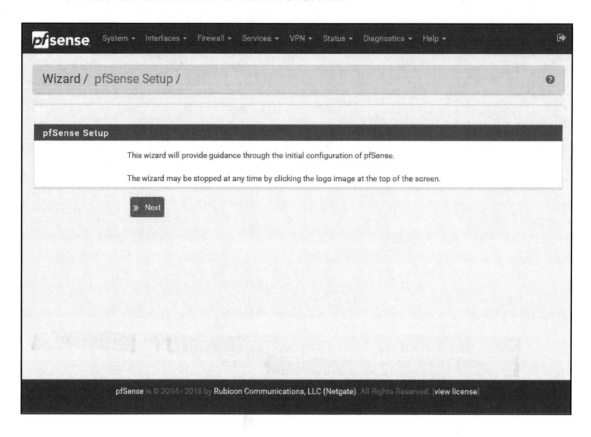

You have successfully installed pfSense server in a virtual platform. Now, you can connect to it over the network via this client system. After the login, pfSense brings you to a helpful Wizard, which will guide you through the rest of the configuration and setup. This wizard is not mandatory. You can skip it at any time and choose to configure your pfSense server manually.

10. Let's go ahead with the wizard for now and perform the initial configuration. Keep clicking on **Next** until you get to the **General Information** tab:

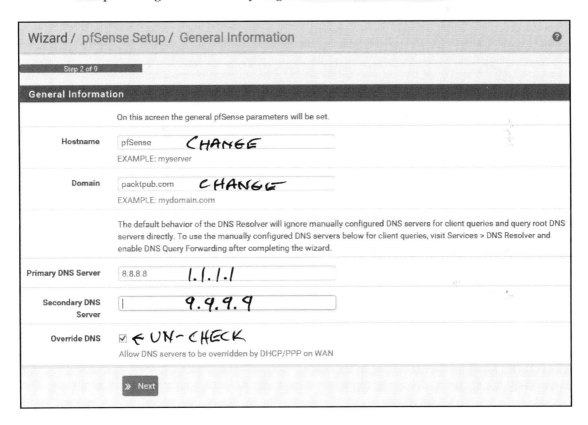

On this screen, you need to enter some general information about your pfSense server.

11. Let's accept the default value for the **Hostname**, which is `pfSense`.

12. Next is the **Domain** name in which pfSense is used, together with the **Hostname**. This will form the **Fully Qualified Domain Name (FQDN)** of the firewall.

13. Let's input `packtpub.com` as the **Domain** name.

14. Next, you are given an opportunity to configure DNS servers for pfSense server. If known, these DNS servers will be used for pfSense itself, as well as for the DHCP clients if the DNS forwarder is off, and for PPTPVPN clients. These may be left blank if you're using a dynamic WAN connection that provides DNS servers, such as PPTP or DHCP. They may also be left blank if the DNS resolved is used in non-forwarding mode. Let's use the Google global DNS server `8.8.8.8`. This last option allows you to override the DNS settings. If a dynamic WAN is present, unchecking this box will make the system use only the servers specified manually and not the ones provided by the ISP. This is especially useful when using open DNS servers for access control or Google Public DNS to work around flaky ISP DNS servers. For now, let's accept the default value for this setting and click on **Next**.

15. For a lot of networking use cases, it is very important that pfSense server has the correct time. To ensure that pfSense server always has the correct time, it can synchronize the system clock with an NTP server. As you may know, Network Time Protocol, or NTP, is a networking protocol for clock synchronization between computer systems over packet-switched, variable latency data networks:

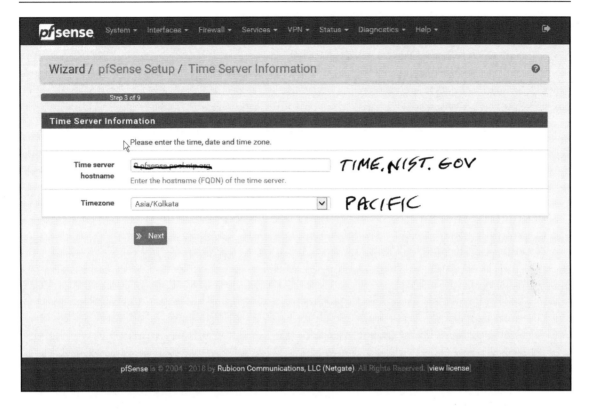

Here, pfSense has provided a default NTP server. Let's accept that and also set the **Timezone**. You need to select the time zone as per your location. In this case, we have selected Asia/Kolkata. Then, you can click on **Next**.

16. You now need to **Configure WAN Interface**. Within the context of pfSense, WAN interface is the connection from your ISP or upstream connections, which allow you to connect to the internet:

17. The **SelectedType DHCP** means that the network interface will get its IP address from a DHCP server. With most small, home office, or even corporate ISPs, they use the DHCP method. You can choose to make it static if your ISP has provided you with a public IP address. If you select **Static**, then you must enter the networking details for your setup, like the public IP Address, Subnet Mask, and Upstream Gateway. pfSense also has support for **PPPoE** and **PPTP** connections. These are for specialized use cases, and we will not discuss them in this book. In this example, let's accept the default value of **DHCP**. You will notice that the setup wizard is smart enough to understand that for **DHCP** setup. You do not need to fill all the fields in the **Static** IP Configuration section. So, the fields shown in the preceding screenshot are disabled if your **SelectedType** is **DHCP**.

18. If you scroll down, you can see that all the default values are good, so you can go ahead and accept them. You can then click on **Next**.

19. Now, you need to **Configure LAN interface**:

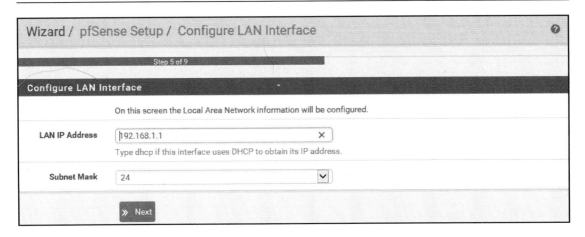

This is the configuration for your internal network. So, you must make sure that these settings are compatible with the rest of your internal network.

pfSense is generally at the periphery of your network boundary, so all your networking equipment such as switches and servers will need to be ready to route their external traffic via this pfSense server. Anyway, these default values of the **LAN IP Address** 192.168.1.1 and the **Subnet Mask** of 24 were already set up by us during the installation phase. So, let's accept them and click on **Next**.

20. Now, you need to **Set Admin WebGUI Password**. WebGUI stands for **Web-based Graphical User Interface**. If you remember, the default admin password that you used to log in to this web console was pfsense. You now have an option to change it here for better security.

21. Let's change the password to a more secure one and then click on **Next**:

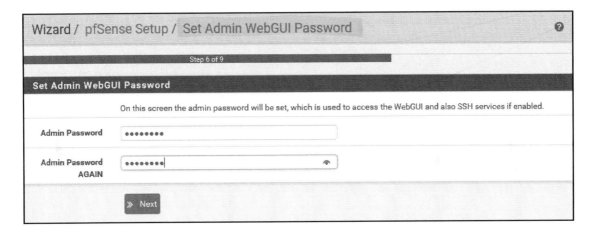

Make sure that you remember the password so that you can log in to the system again. And that's it. The wizard has finished.

Mind you, pfSense has worked really hard to make the initial configuration as easy and as painless as possible. But don't let this simplicity fool you. There is a plethora of settings you can tweak in pfSense to make it behave exactly the way you want. We'll go over these settings in the upcoming sections.

pfSense has now been configured through the WebGUI.

22. Click on **Reload** to save all of the configuration settings:

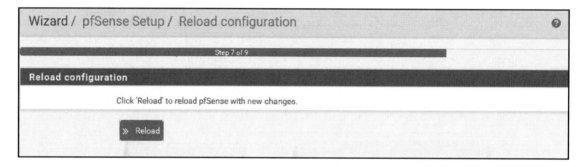

pfSense will save the configuration and reload itself:

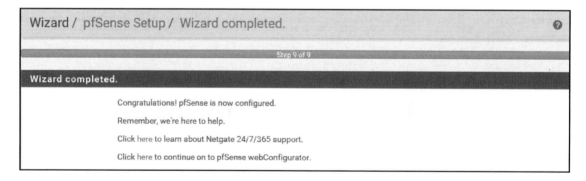

Great! The configuration is now complete and changes have been saved.

23. Click on the second link to navigate to the main **pfSense webConfigurator** dashboard:

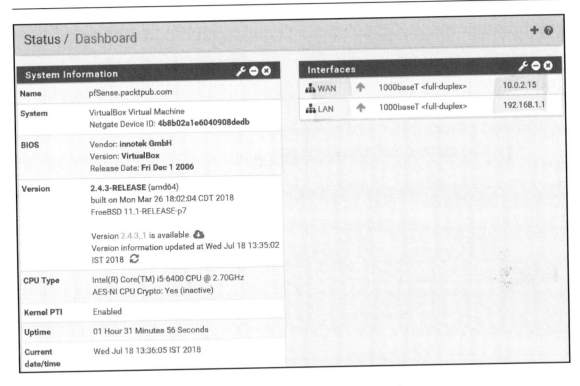

This is the main Dashboard for this pfSense server, where you can see an overview of the pfSense system. The domain **Name** is `pfSense.packtpub.com`. pfSense's **Version** is **2.4.3-RELEASE(amd64)**. **Uptime** is how long this pfSense server has been up. pfSense is so stable and robust, and we have seen it run for months and even years without any downtime.

On the right-hand side, you can see that all the network interfaces are also listed along with the names and current status. As you can see, we have two interfaces. One is attached to a WAN connection and the second one is attached to a LAN connection. Both of them are in an up state, indicated by the green up arrow. A whole bunch of vital information about this pfSense server is available right on the central dashboard of pfSense. If you're wondering how this pfSense WebGUI console is related to the pfSense server you installed, let's have a quick peek at the server.

You'll notice that it has detected that the admin account has logged in to the WebGUI from the IP address `192.168.1.2`:

```
Message from syslogd@pfSense at Jul 18 08:04:53 ...
pfSense php-fpm[333]: /index.php: Successful login for user 'admin' from: 192.16
8.1.2
```

pfSense WebGUI walkthrough

You just saw the main dashboard of the pfSense WebGUI interface, but that is just us scratching the surface. Now, let's walk through the pfSense WebGUI interface and check out what else it has to offer.

Okay, now, back in the pfSense WebGUI dashboard, let's explore this:

1. Click on **System** and then on **Advanced**:

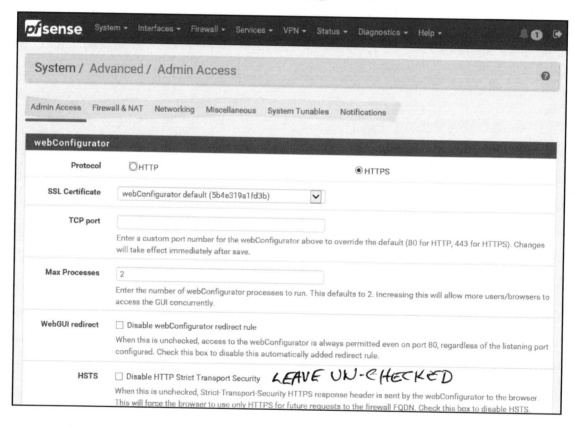

There are multiple tabs here with different information:

- The **Admin Access** tab contains settings for the WebGUI such as the **Protocol** (**HTTP** or **HTTPS**) and port, security settings for management, SSH daemon settings, serial console settings, and console options
- **Firewall & NAT** contains settings that tweak the behavior of the firewall, such as fragmentation, optimization algorithms, and state table settings

- **Networking** contains settings for IPv6 and various network interface settings, such as hardware, checksums, device polling, and ARP message suppression
- **Miscellaneous** contains settings that do not fit into the other categories
- **System Tunables** contains an interface to manage various FreeBSD system values that tweak different system behavior
- **Notifications** control how the system will notify administrators when an alert happens

The advanced settings available here do not normally need adjusting on a typical setup. These here are for additional tweaking or for those who need the functionality given. We do not need to change anything here, so let's move on.

2. Click on **System** again and then on **Cert. Manager**:

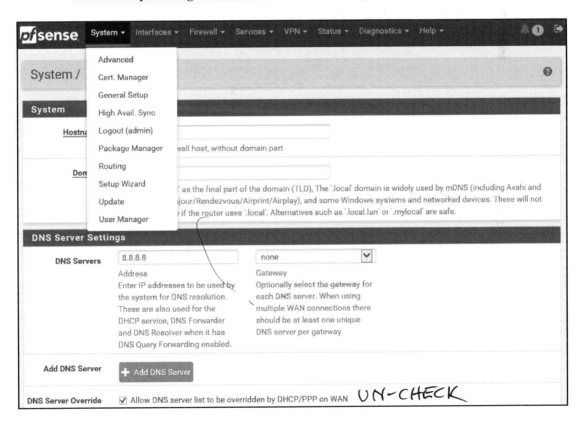

pfSense includes a central certificate manager under **System** and **Cert. Manager**. This central certificate management takes the place of several other locations inside pfSense, which you can use to acquire certificates we entered directly into their configurations, such as for HTTPS SSL access to the WebGUI, OpenVPNPKI certificate management, and IPsec certificate management. Each set of certificates is bound to a certificate authority. These are managed from the Certificate Authority tab. Certificates are managed on the **Certificates** tab. **Certificate Revocation Lists** (**CRL**s) control which certificates are valid for a given CA. If a certificate is compromised in some way or is invalidated, it can be added to a CRL and that CRL may be selected for use by an OpenVPN server. Then, the OpenVPN client using that certificate will no longer be allowed to connect. Certificate revocation lists are managed from the **Certificate Revocation** tab.

3. Click on **System** and then on **General Setup**:

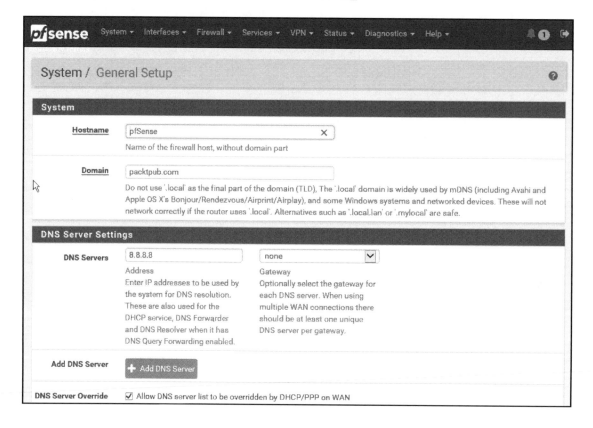

4. You can scroll down and look at all the general setup settings available. These are more or less the same settings which you set while going through the configuration wizard.
   Similarly, the following are the other options available under the **System** menu:

- **High Avail. Sync**: High Avail. Sync which can enable you to deploy multiple instances of pfSense and configure them in a high availability mode. You can also log out of your active session from the WebGUI.
- **Package Manager**: Package Manager used to install and maintain packages on a pfSense firewall.
- **Routing**: Routing enables you to set up gateways and gateway groups. A gateway is a system through which pfSense can reach the internet or another network. So, if multiple LANs are in use, or if there are multiple paths to the internet via different gateways, the associated gateways must be defined. Gateways must also be assigned for networks that are reachable via static routes.
- **Setup Wizard**: The Setup Wizard will enable you to reset your configurations for your pfSense server.
- **Update**: This menu will allow you to update your pfSense server with the latest version of the software.
- **User Manager**: Let's click on it and explore further. In pfSense, user management has been centralized under this option.

This takes the place of the individual user management and access to server settings that used to be available under various subsystems. Users are managed at the list view on the Users tab. The **admin** user cannot be deleted, and its username cannot be changed. You can see this **admin** account in the following screenshot. The standard practice is to create at least one other user. So, let's do that.

5. Click on the **Add** button to add another user:

6. Enter a **Username** and **Password**. Let's call this new user `packt`. Repeat the password to confirm.

7. The next setting is **Group membership**. pfSense has this notion of role-based security. Users can be a member of groups or roles, which can have different access rights. By default, there are two groups, namely all users and **admins**. Members of the **admins** group have full access to the WebGUI. For now, let's assign **admins** group to this new user. For production environments, of course, you should consider setting up different groups with more fine-grained permissions. Click on the **Move to Member of list** button and then on the **Save** button.

You've now created a new pfSense user:

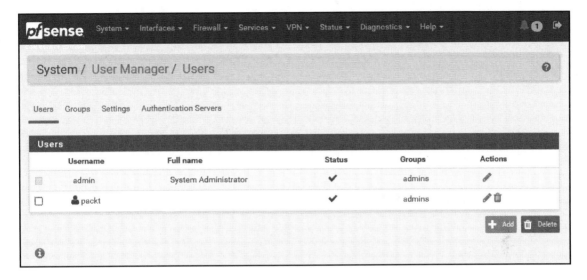

The question that comes to mind naturally is, why create a user account when you already have an **admin** account? Well, the answer is simple, for security purposes!

The **admin** account has far-reaching privileges to change the entire configuration of the pfSense server. Using an **admin** account makes you vulnerable to attacks. If this account is compromised in any way, then any malicious hacker can make changes to pfSense, whereas, if you are using a regular user account and a weakly privileged account is compromised in any way, you wouldn't have much to worry about. And since **admin** is a public account in pfSense, anyone can try a brute force dictionary attack to crack the password and gain access to your pfSense server. For that reason, the best practice is to disable the default **admin** account and set up other accounts for managing your pfSense server. This is called **security by obscurity**.

8. All you need to do is select the edit icon for the **admin** user and select the **This user cannot login** checkbox:

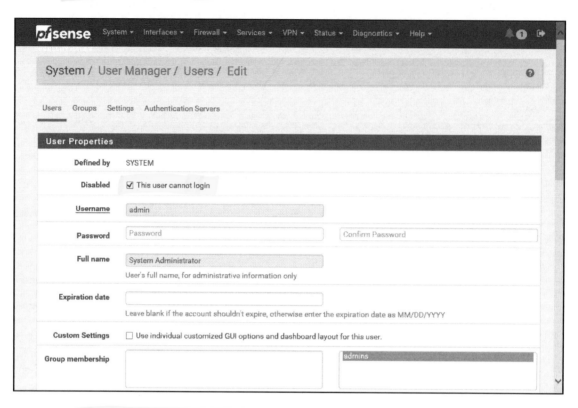

9. Save the settings and log out from the account.

When you try to log in again, you will see that you do not have access to log in. So with that, effectively, you have reduced the attack surface area for hackers to try and guess the password and log in to your pfSense server. Now, let's try to log in using the new `packt` user account.

You can see that it works. Every time you log in to the console, pfSense automatically runs a query for an updated version of the software. If it finds an updated version, it will inform you right here.

You can just click on this version link to upgrade your pfSense server. It's easy as pie. It is recommended that you keep your pfSense software up to date, unless there is a very good reason to defer the upgrades.

10. To confirm that the admin has been disabled, go to the **System** drop-down menu option and select **User Manager**:

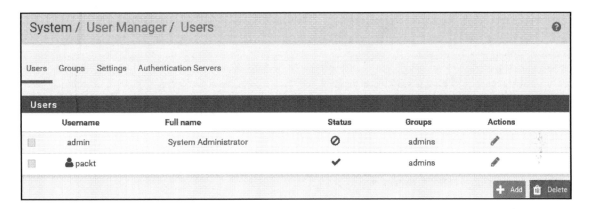

As you can see, here, **admin** is disabled. Instead of **admin**, we are using the user account **packt** for security purposes.

11. Let's move on to the **Interfaces** drop-down. There are two interfaces: LAN and WAN. Select WAN and scroll down to review all the settings configured for this interface. As you can see, pfSense gives you a lot of power to tweak the settings on each interface. Let's take a quick peek at the second interface, which is the **LAN** interface:

LAN		
General Options		
Enable	☑ Enable DHCP server on LAN interface	
BOOTP	☐ Ignore BOOTP queries	
Deny unknown clients	☐ Only the clients defined below will get DHCP leases from this server.	
Ignore denied clients	☐ Denied clients will be ignored rather than rejected.	
	This option is not compatible with failover and cannot be enabled when a Failover Peer IP address is configured.	
Ignore client identifiers	☐ If a client includes a unique identifier in its DHCP request, that UID will not be recorded in its lease.	
	This option may be useful when a client can dual boot using different client identifiers but the same hardware (MAC) address. Note that the resulting server behavior violates the official DHCP specification.	
Subnet	192.168.1.0	
Subnet mask	255.255.255.0	
Available range	192.168.1.1 - 192.168.1.254	
Range	192.168.1.100	192.168.1.199
	From	To

You will see information such as IP Address and **Subnet mask**.

12. The next tab is **Firewall**. Click on it. You can configure NAT, Traffic Shaper, Virtual IPs, and so forth from here.

13. From the **Services** tab, you can select all the services provided by pfSense, such as DHCP Server, DHCP Relay, DNS Resolver, and Dynamic DNS.

14. Under the **VPN** menu, you can configure the various types of support VPN connectivity options. You have IPsec, OpenVPN, and L2TP. If you click on the **Status** tab, you can see a lot of other information about various services running on the pfSense server. This applies for the **Diagnostics**, **Gold**, and **Help** tabs.

This was a high-level overview of the pfSense WebGUI configuration console. We will visit many of these options and settings in the upcoming demos but this quick overview should give you an idea of how flexible and feature-rich pfSense really is.

Configuring pfSense as a DHCP server

Now that you are familiar with the pfSense interface, let's see how to configure the various pfSense services, starting with the DHCP server:

1. Let's open the WebGUI administration console for the pfSense server. Now, click on the **Services** menu located on the top toolbar and then click on the DHCP Server.

   The DHCP Server in pfSense will hand out addresses to DHCP clients, and automatically configure them for network access.

   By default, the DHCP server is enabled on the LAN interface. In case you can see that the DHCP server is not enabled in your instance of pfSense, you can check the box to enable it, as shown in the previous screenshot.

   Using the **Deny unknown clients** option, DHCP access can be prevented for any client which is not included in the list at the bottom of the page. Similarly, static ARP may also be enabled to further restrict access, so that only the clients who are listed can talk to the pfSense router. There are other options such as **Subnet** and **Subnet mask**. These will be assigned to the clients when they get a unique dynamic IP address from the DHCP server. Currently, the **Subnet** is set to 192.168.1.0 and the **Subnet mask** is set to 255.255.255.0. By default, the DHCP server automatically sets the DHCP address range. The DHCP address range is the range of IP addresses that the DHCP server can assign to network devices. IP addresses outside of the DHCP address range are reserved for statically addressed computers. You can see the available range of IP addresses, which is 192.168.1.1 to 192.168.1.254. So, that is 255 IP addresses that you can have in your internal network. In most cases, this is more than enough; however, if you have more devices in a larger network, you can change the **Subnet mask** to get a larger range.

2. You can also configure the actual range to be different than the entire available IP address range. That way, you can exclude some IP addresses from the dynamic pool, and use them for static IP allocations: ~ *PRINTER*

Servers	
WINS servers	WINS Server 1
	WINS Server 2
DNS servers	192.168.1.1
	DNS Server 2
	DNS Server 3
	DNS Server 4
	Leave blank to use the system default DNS servers: this interface's IP if DNS Forwarder or Resolver is enabled, otherwise the servers configured on the System / General Setup page.

Other Options	
Gateway	192.168.1.1
	The default is to use the IP on this interface of the firewall as the gateway. Specify an alternate gateway here if this is not the correct gateway for the network. Type "none" for no gateway assignment.
Domain name	packtpub.com
	The default is to use the domain name of this system as the default domain name provided by DHCP. An alternate domain name may be specified here.
Domain search list	
	The DHCP server can optionally provide a domain search list. Use the semicolon character as separator.

You can also set some more options. DHCP servers can be configured to provide optional data that fully configures TCP/IP on a client. Some of the most common DHCP option types configured and distributed by the DHCP server during leases include the default gateway, router, and DNS parameters. Even though pfSense is smart enough to assign the correct values based on the usual configuration, you can specify specific options here. For instance, let's set the first DNS server field to **192.168.1.1**, which is basically pointing the DNS to this pfSense server.

3. In the **Gateway** field, let's also enter 192.168.1.1, which once again will assign this pfSense server as the default gateway to the DHCP clients. In the **Domain name** field, enter packtpub.com. Then, click on **Save**. Here, you will get the confirmation message.

The DHCP server is now configured. Great!

Now, let's play around with the networking settings for this Windows Server client system and observe what effect these pfSense DHCP changes had on the clients:

1. Open the **Network and Sharing Center** in the Windows 2012 Server client.
2. Click on the **Change adapter settings** link.
3. Double-click on **Ethernet0** and then click on **Properties**. Here, double-click on IPv4 settings. Originally, we'd assigned the static IP address of 192.168.1.2 to the server. Along with that, we also specified the other settings for the DNS and Default gateway explicitly, but now, we can get these settings from the DHCP server.
4. Select the **Obtain an IP address automatically** option and also select the **Obtain DNS server address automatically** option:

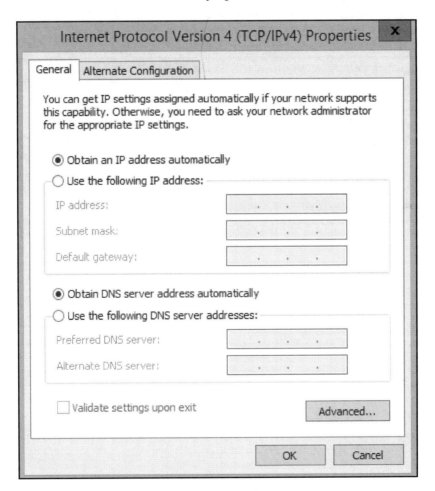

Since the DHCP server has been configured to pass on all these options directly to the clients, we do not need to specify them here individually for any device on the network. That is the true benefit of a DHCP server.

5. Click on **OK** and close the windows.
6. Now, let's check the IP address of the client machine. It should receive a new IP address from the DHCP server. Open the Command Prompt and execute the following command:

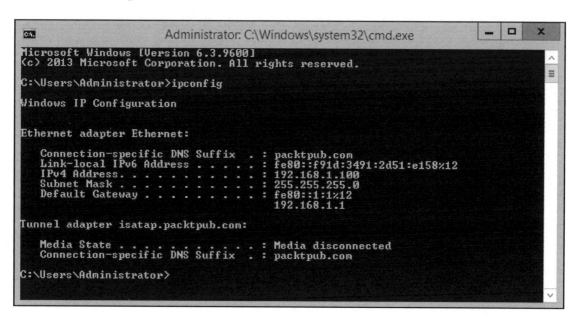

As you can see, the new IP address assigned to this system is `192.168.1.100`.

The rest of the settings have also been assigned correctly to this client machine. This is exactly what we expected. So, excellent! You have now finished configuring the DHCP server.

Next, let's add another client to the same LAN network. Here, we have another virtual machine running Windows 7:

1. Let's open Network Connections. This system belongs to the same network, but, as you can see, the LAN network adapter is disabled. Let's enable it.
2. Right-click on the icon and select **Enable**. This adapter has already been set up to get a dynamic IP address for the DHCP server. This adapter is connected and it should have received a new IP address. Let's check it.
3. So, open the Command Prompt and execute the `ipconfig` command again:

```
C:\Windows\system32\cmd.exe

Microsoft Windows [Version 6.1.7601]
Copyright (c) 2009 Microsoft Corporation.  All rights reserved.

C:\Users\packt>ipconfig

Windows IP Configuration


Ethernet adapter Local Area Connection:

   Connection-specific DNS Suffix  . : packtpub.com
   Link-local IPv6 Address . . . . . : fe80::780c:d57c:aef3:2b13%11
   IPv4 Address. . . . . . . . . . . : 192.168.1.101
   Subnet Mask . . . . . . . . . . . : 255.255.255.0
   Default Gateway . . . . . . . . . : fe80::1:1%11
                                       192.168.1.1

Tunnel adapter isatap.packtpub.com:

   Media State . . . . . . . . . . . : Media disconnected
   Connection-specific DNS Suffix  . : packtpub.com

C:\Users\packt>
```

The IP address is `192.168.1.101` and all other networking settings are also as per expectations. If you check the range from the web browser, the IP address is within the specified range for this DHCP server.

4. Now, let's check how you can control the DHCP server. For that, click on **Status** on the top toolbar and then on **Services**. Here, you can see all the services running on this pfSense system:

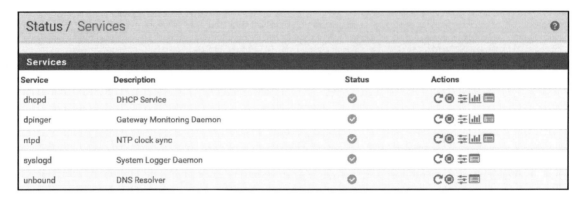

The first one is DHCP. You can see that the DHCP service is currently running.

5. Let's stop the service from the actions panel. Click on the **Stop** icon:

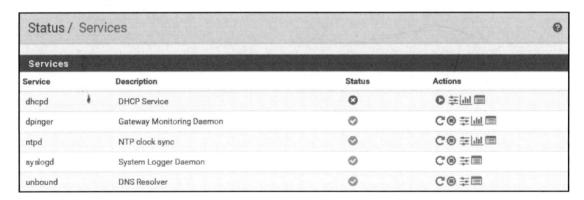

The DHCP service has been stopped. There are other options in the panel such as **Related settings** and **Related status**.

6. If you click on status, you can see that the DHCP Pool range is between IP addresses `192.168.1.100` and `192.168.1.199`:

Status / DHCP Leases

Leases

	IP address	MAC address	Hostname	Description	Start	End	Online	Lease Type	Actions
⊘	192.168.1.101	08:00:27:83:b9:21	packt-PC		2018/07/18 11:31:34	2018/07/18 13:31:34	online	active	⊞⊡
⊘	192.168.1.100	08:00:27:ff:a2:36	WIN-K9O84G6EDIO		2018/07/18 10:54:30	2018/07/18 12:54:30	online	active	⊞⊡

Leases in Use

Interface	Pool Start	Pool End	# of leases in use
LAN	192.168.1.100	192.168.1.199	2

➕ Show all configured leases

7. Let's go back and restart the DHCP server. The service is now running. Now, go to the client system and try to renew the IP address.

8. Right-click on the LAN connection and select **Disable** and then again click **Enable** to enable it. This will reset the adapter and also force it to renew its IP address. Okay, now, the adapter has changed the state and it is trying to identify its network.

9. Once it's done identifying, let's switch to the Command Prompt and execute `ipconfig` again:

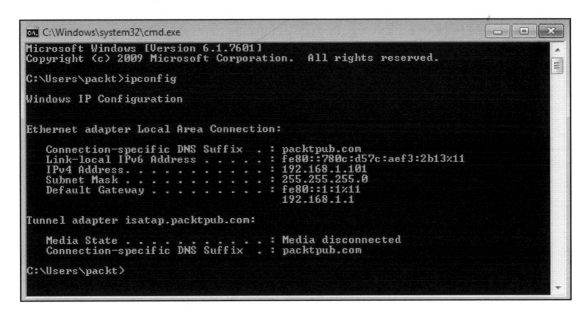

You can see that the system has the same IP address. Note that since we reset the adapter, this new IP address was fetched again from the DHCP server. The IP address now matches. The **Services** section shows that the DHCP server is running.

10. From the actions panel, click on **Related settings**:

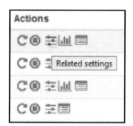

This will lead you to the same DHCP server settings page you visited earlier. You can modify many settings here such as **Default lease time**, **Dynamic DNS**, and **NTP, TFTP, LDAP**, and **Network Booting**.

11. Let's go back to the **Status** page. Click on **Status** and then on **DHCP Leases**. Here, you can see the IP address lease assigned to the Windows 7 client system:

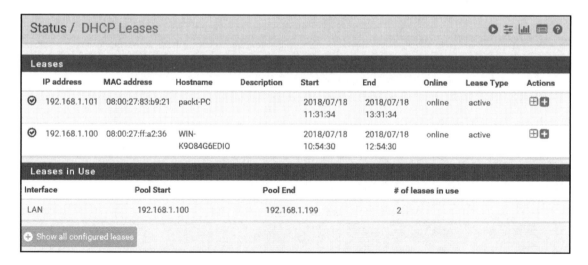

The MAC address for that system is also listed here. You can always verify this information.

12. Let's get back to the Command Prompt and execute the `ipconfig` /All
command. This will list all the details about the networking setup on the system:

```
C:\Users\packt>ipconfig /all

Windows IP Configuration

    Host Name . . . . . . . . . . . . : packt-PC
    Primary Dns Suffix  . . . . . . . :
    Node Type . . . . . . . . . . . . : Hybrid
    IP Routing Enabled. . . . . . . . : No
    WINS Proxy Enabled. . . . . . . . : No
    DNS Suffix Search List. . . . . . : packtpub.com

Ethernet adapter Local Area Connection:

    Connection-specific DNS Suffix  . : packtpub.com
    Description . . . . . . . . . . . : Intel(R) PRO/1000 MT Desktop Adapter
    Physical Address. . . . . . . . . : 08-00-27-83-B9-21
    DHCP Enabled. . . . . . . . . . . : Yes
    Autoconfiguration Enabled . . . . : Yes
    Link-local IPv6 Address . . . . . : fe80::780c:d57c:aef3:2b13%11(Preferred)
    IPv4 Address. . . . . . . . . . . : 192.168.1.101(Preferred)
    Subnet Mask . . . . . . . . . . . : 255.255.255.0
    Lease Obtained. . . . . . . . . . : 18 July 2018 17:07:27
    Lease Expires . . . . . . . . . . : 18 July 2018 19:01:35
    Default Gateway . . . . . . . . . : fe80::1:1%11
                                        192.168.1.1
    DHCP Server . . . . . . . . . . . : 192.168.1.1
    DHCPv6 IAID . . . . . . . . . . . : 235405351
    DHCPv6 Client DUID. . . . . . . . : 00-01-00-01-22-E0-DC-5A-08-00-27-83-B9-21

    DNS Servers . . . . . . . . . . . : 192.168.1.1
    NetBIOS over Tcpip. . . . . . . . : Enabled

Tunnel adapter isatap.packtpub.com:

    Media State . . . . . . . . . . . : Media disconnected
    Connection-specific DNS Suffix  . : packtpub.com
    Description . . . . . . . . . . . : Microsoft ISATAP Adapter
    Physical Address. . . . . . . . . : 00-00-00-00-00-00-00-E0
    DHCP Enabled. . . . . . . . . . . : No
    Autoconfiguration Enabled . . . . : Yes
```

All the details of the IP and MAC addresses are listed here. A MAC address is given to a network adapter when it is manufactured. It is hardwired or hard-coded onto your computer's network interface card and it's unique to it. Let's take a note of this MAC address. It starts with 80 and ends with 21. These are all hexadecimal numbers. Now, let's compare that MAC address to the one listed on the IP address **Lease Status** page and verify it. This MAC address is the same as the client machine. The Host Name is packt-PC.

13. You can verify this by going to **Start**, right-clicking on **Computer**, and selecting **Properties**:

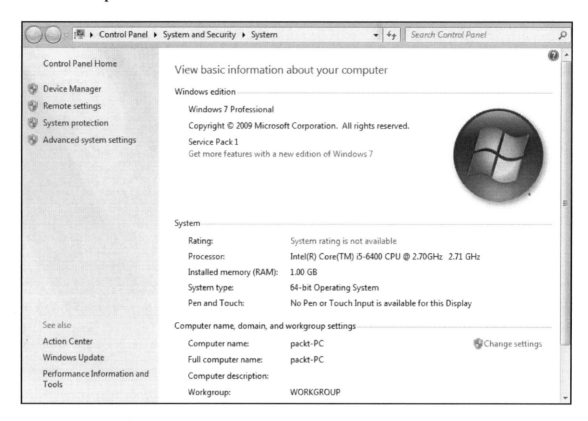

As you can see here, the **Computer name** is also **packt-PC**.

In the previous **DHCP Lease** tab, you can also see the **Start** time and the **End** time. This is the start and end date of the IP address lease.

When this lease expires, the DHCP server is responsible for assigning a new IP address from the available pool to the clients. You have many other features available here.

14. You can click on this **Log** icon at the top right corner, where you can view all the log entries:

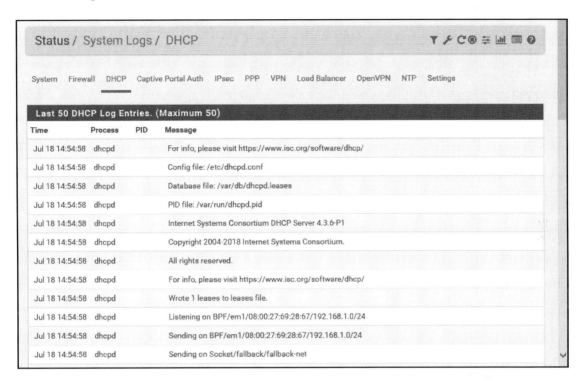

The preceding screenshot shows detailed log entries for the DHCP server. You can see the inner workings of the DHCP server from here.

Here, the client machine discovered the DHCP server:

```
Jul 18 17:01:34    dhcpd                    DHCPOFFER on 192.168.1.101 to 08:00:27:83:b9:21 (packt-PC) via em1
```

The DHCP server offers a lease to the client. Finally, the selected DHCP server acknowledges the client DHCP request for the IP address by sending a **DHCPACK** packet:

```
Jul 18 17:01:34    dhcpd                    DHCPACK on 192.168.1.101 to 08:00:27:83:b9:21 (packt-PC) via em1
```

This time, the server also forwards any optional configuration parameters. Upon receipt of the **DHCPACK**, the client can participate in the TCP/IP network, and complete its system startup.

So, we just saw a very detailed walkthrough of setting up a DHCP server on pfSense.

Summary

Let's recap some of the key points that we covered in this chapter. You learned all about what pfSense is, its key features, advantages, and why it's such a great tool. Next, you went through a series of demonstrations that gave you a practical insight into installing pfSense on your network infrastructure. Next, you learned how to configure pfSense and got a walkthrough of the pfSense WebGUI and all the tasks you can perform. Finally, you learned about configuring pfSense as a DHCP server.

In the next chapter, you will learn about the firewall features of pfSense.

pfSense as a Firewall 2

In the previous chapter, you got familiar with pfSense and the features provided by it. You also went through the process of installing and configuring pfSense, and you subsequently configured your pfSense server as a DHCP server. A firewall is a software or hardware device that protects your computer from being attacked over the internet by hackers, viruses, and worms. This may occur either on a large corporate network, or simply on a small home network. Both have the same security issues. With the level of threats floating around on the internet, the firewall has become an essential part of any network, large or small. pfSense is a very robust, secure, and flexible firewall. In this chapter, you will learn how to configure pfSense as a firewall. You'll also learn how to create and manage multiple firewall rules.

Here are some of the key learning objectives of this chapter. First, you will learn all about what firewalls are, their key functions, and importance. Next, you'll go through a series of demonstrations that will give you a practical insight into configuring pfSense as a firewall. And, last but not least, you will learn to set up firewall rules for multiple LANs. And you'll also learn how to manage these firewall rules using pfSense. So, let's get going.

What is a firewall?

A firewall is a hardware or software based network security system that uses rules to control incoming and outgoing network traffic. It basically acts as a barrier between a trusted network and an untrusted network. A firewall controls access to the resources of a network through a positive control model. What this means is that only the traffic defined in the firewall policy is allowed onto the network, and all other traffic is denied. It filters traffic by source and destination IP, protocols, source, and destination ports for both TCP and UDP traffic. It also limits simultaneous connection on a rule basis.

Now, let's take a look at the following diagram and see how pfSense can act as a firewall:

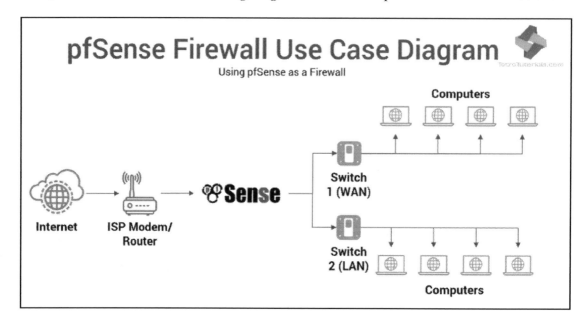

Consider that there is an external cloud network, which represents the **Internet**. Next, you have an **ISP** connection device, such as a cable modem, an ADSL modem, or something similar, that connects your internal network and pfSense system to the internet. There are two network ports both leading to two switches. Let's say one is a **WAN** port and the other is a **LAN** port. Each of these has numerous endpoints or devices connected to that segment of the **LAN**, which could be laptops or desktops. Whenever any traffic tries to pass to the **WAN**, it will go through pfSense, and then be filtered to the correct route.

Now let's add another layer of complexity:

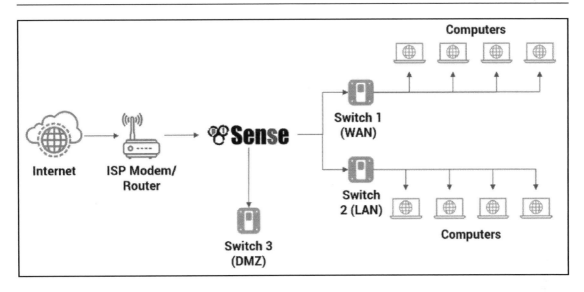

Say there is an additional **LAN** segment added, which could be attached to a third network interface within the pfSense server. This will be the second **LAN** interface. Say this new **LAN** segment hosts some other devices or servers, which need to be isolated from the first **LAN** segment. This is a typical case when you need to host external servers in a different **LAN** segment, which may behave like a **DMZ**. In the context of computer security and firewalling, a **DMZ**, or **De-Militarized Zone**, is a physical or logical subnetwork that contains and exposes an organization's external-facing services to an untrusted network - usually a larger network, such as the **Internet**. The purpose of a **DMZ** is to add an additional layer of security to an organization's local area network, or **LAN**. An external network node can access only what is exposed in the **DMZ**, while the rest of the organization's network is firewalled. A **DMZ** functions as a small isolated network, positioned between the Internet and the private network. The term is derived from the term, well, de-militarized zone, an area between nation states in which military operation is not permitted. In this type of setup, you will set the pfSense firewall rules to isolate the **LAN** and **DMZ** networks and not any traffic to overlap with each other. Assume that **Switch 3** is the **DMZ**, and that **Switch 2** is the internal **LAN** zone, and all the traffic is being passed through the pfSense server.

Let's quickly review the environment setup once again:

- The main pfSense server has been installed on a virtual machine.
- It has three network interfaces.
- The WAN interface will represent the ISP internet connection.
- LAN 1 will represent the internal LAN network. We have a Windows Server 2012 R2 machine in this LAN network.
- LAN 2 will represent a DMZ network. And the Windows 7 client will reside on this DMZ network.
- All these machines have been created and launched on VirtualBox.

Now that you have all the prerequisites in place, let's see how to configure pfSense as a firewall.

Configuring pfSense as a firewall

Let's connect to the pfSense server via a browser:

1. Navigate to 192.168.1.1, which is the internal LAN IP address for the pfSense server.
2. Enter the credentials to log in to the pfSense server. Here, the **admin** user has logged in successfully.

   We allocated an additional network interface to the virtual machine, but have not configured it yet. So, let's take care of that now.

3. Click Interfaces on the top toolbar, and select **LAN2**. There you can configure the LAN2 with a static IP address as you did for earlier LAN interface we configured previously.
4. After setting the configurations for **LAN2**, let's click the **Apply Changes** button to save the configuration. You can see that the changes have been successfully saved. Let's go back to the main pfSense **Dashboard**:

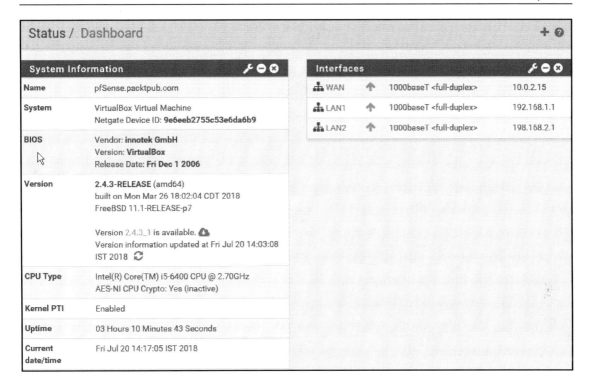

And you will see that **LAN2** is up and running with an IP address of
192.168.2.1. This is a separate **LAN2** segment that is different from **LAN1**. The
WAN interface has a public IP address of 10.0.2.15. There are two segments in
the private network: **LAN1** and **LAN2**.

5. Note that we have renamed **LAN** to **LAN1** for this demonstration from the **General Configuration** tab in the **Interfaces** menu:

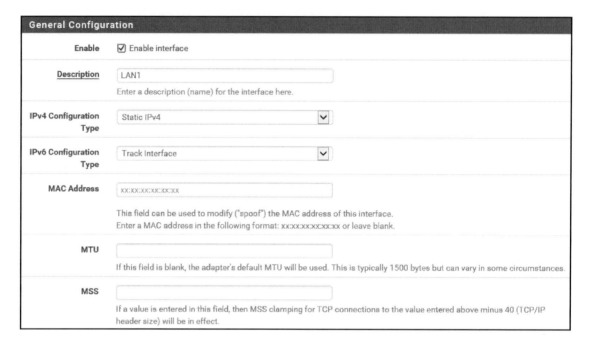

The key focus of this demo is on configuring pfSense as a firewall.

6. To do this, click **System** and select **Advanced**. You will see the **Admin Access**
    tab, which is related to general admin user access settings:

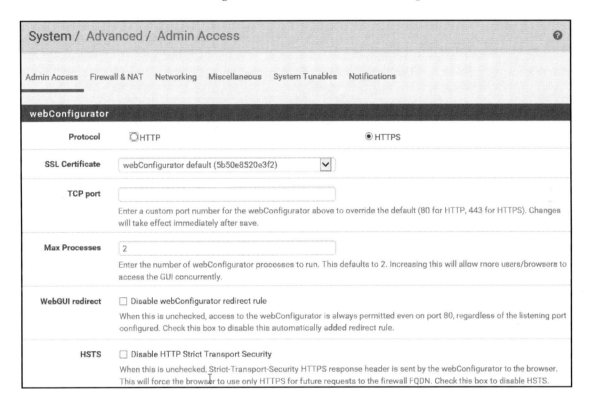

Here, the **webConfigurator** has been set up to serve the pages on **HTTPS**. That is the reason why this portal is accessible only on **HTTPS**. And if you recall, that is the reason you got an SSL certificate warning earlier.

7. Anyway, let's switch to the **Firewall & NAT** tab:

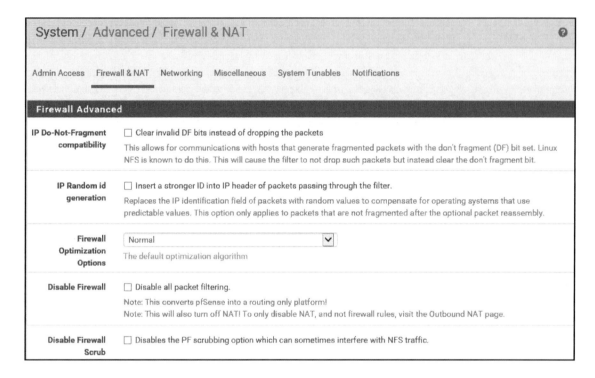

This section contains settings that tweak the behavior of the firewall, such as fragmentation, optimization algorithms, and state table settings. One of these options is called **Disable Firewall**. Make sure that this option is unchecked. If this option is checked then pfSense will only act as a router, and all its firewall features, including NAT, will be disabled. Now, pfSense, being the flexible platform it is, does provide options for you to only disable NAT, which you can do by visiting the Outbound NAT page. The link to that page is provided at the end of the **Disable Firewall** section.

But for now, you must uncheck the **Disable Firewall** checkbox to ensure the firewall functionality is available.

8. Click **Save** to make sure any changes are saved.

Enabling the firewall is that easy in pfSense. But the more involved part is configuring the firewall rules. So, we'll take care of that next.

Setting up firewall rules

In the previous section, we enabled the firewall functionality within pfSense. Now it is time to configure firewall rules:

1. Back in the pfSense WebGUI console, to set up rules for the firewall go to the **Firewall** menu and then click **Rules.** Firewall rules are configured for each network interface. The following screenshot shows the **WAN** tab:

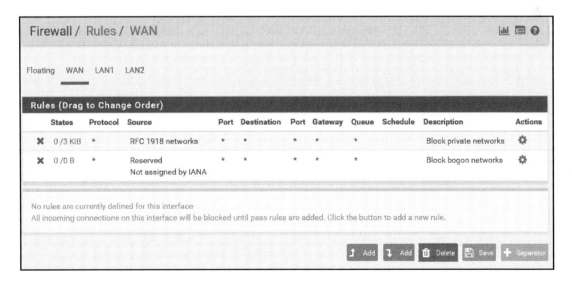

As you can see, pfSense is flexible enough to allow for firewall rules for each individual network, rather than enforcing these rules globally. Moreover, the rules follow a specific order. The rules on these tabs process traffic in an inbound direction and are processed from the top down, stopping at the first match. Where no user-configured firewall rules match, the traffic is denied. The firewall rules on the LAN interface, allowing the LAN subnet to access any destination, are implemented by pfSense by default. On the firewall rules page, there is a tab for each interface, plus a tab for each active VPN type as seen in the previous screenshot for example, IPsec, OpenVPN, and PPTP. And there is a tab for **Floating** rules, which contains more advanced rules that apply to multiple interfaces and directions. Here, you have multiple tabs showing the three interfaces: **WAN**, **LAN1**, and **LAN2**. Since you just added the **LAN2** section, it is devoid of any firewall rules, while **LAN1** and **WAN** have some rules defined.

Since **WAN** is currently being used to route traffic to the internet, any modifications could cause interruptions in the internet connection itself. So, for this instance let's focus on **LAN1** and **LAN2**.

2. Open the **LAN1** tab:

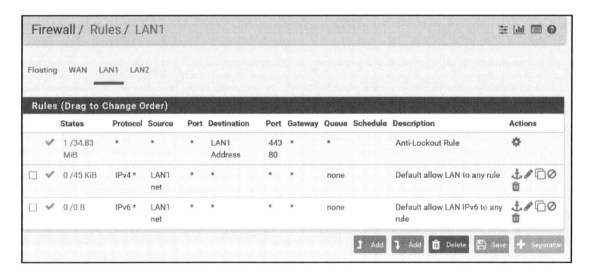

There are three rules defined. As you have seen in the **WAN** tab screenshot, there are two default rules defined there.

These firewall rules control what traffic is allowed in and out of a connected network behind the firewall. So, there's not much to control here, as far as firewall rules are concerned. You will primarily work with **LAN1** and **LAN2** interfaces to define rules.

Let's first look into the **LAN1** tab. Here you can see three default rules. The first rule is the **Anti-Lockout Rule** for ports **443** and **80**. This rule was established to enable access to the pfSense server's WebGUI in the case of any misconfiguration in the IP filter or the firewall rules. pfSense is secure by default. So, without even configuring any explicit rules yourself, you will see some rules have already been implemented for us. The default configuration of pfSense allows access to the web-based GUI management console from any machine on the LAN. And to secure the network by default, it also denies any traffic inbound from outside the local network. For the first rule, you can see its mentioned **Anti-Lockout Rule**. What is this? Well, this rule is implemented by pfSense and is enabled by default. This **Anti-Lockout Rule** prevents other firewall rules from being configured in a way that will lock the user out of the WebGUI administration console.

> It is very important that when you configure rules for your firewall, you do not delete the **Anti-Lockout Rule** on the LAN interface. Deleting this rule will lock you out of the pfSense WebGUI.

The other two rules are **Default allow LAN to any rule** for **IPv4** and the **Default allow LAN IPv6 to any rule**. You will notice that the protocol allowed for each of these rules. The source is set to **LAN1** for both these rules. And this applies to network packets on any port for any destination gateway, and so on. So basically, these rules will allow outgoing traffic from the **LAN1** network segment to any target server, over any network port, and via any gateway. These are pretty liberal rules, which allow users to access any public resource on the internet. But you will notice there is no incoming rule defined where the source could be an external source. Hence, pfSense is secured by default. To make it even more secure, let's delete the two default rules by clicking the bin icon under **Actions**:

3. Click **OK**. The rule has been deleted, but you still need to save the changes.

4. Click the **Apply Changes** button to save all changes. Whenever you apply changes, you get an option to **Monitor** the status:

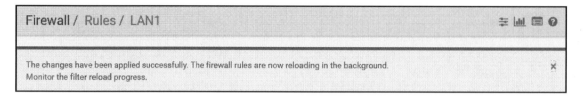

Here, you further diagnose the configuration changes for pfSense. If you check, you will see the status is currently **Done**. The filter rules have been reloaded, which means all the changes were successfully saved and pfSense has reloaded the freshly configured rules.

5. Let's get back to the **Firewall Rules** page. Follow the same process to delete the other default rule.

Before you create new rules, there is one important point to remember. Whenever there are no rules, it means that any outgoing traffic from the **LAN1** interface is blocked by default. And so the client machines will not be able to connect to the internet or external servers. Let's test this.

6. Let's head over to the Windows 7 client. Open a browser window and try to search for google.com. Meanwhile, also open the Command Prompt and enter the following command:

```
ping 192.168.1.1 -t
```

Here is the output:

```
C:\Windows\system32\cmd.exe - ping 192.168.1.1 -t

Tunnel adapter isatap.packtpub.com:

   Media State . . . . . . . . . . . : Media disconnected
   Connection-specific DNS Suffix  . : packtpub.com

C:\Users\packt>ping 192.168.1.1 -t

Pinging 192.168.1.1 with 32 bytes of data:
Request timed out.
Request timed out.
Request timed out.
```

As you can see, there is no response as all outgoing traffic on any protocol or port is blocked on the server.

7. Now, in the previous section, you learned about firewall settings. Let's see what happens if we disable the firewall on this LAN.

8. Click **System** and then click **Advanced**.

9. Select and enable the **Disable all packet filtering** option. Then click the **Save** button to save the changes.

10. Go back to the Command Prompt:

```
C:\Windows\system32\cmd.exe - ping 192.168.1.1 -t
Request timed out.
Request timed out.
Request timed out.
Request timed out.
Request timed out.
Request timed out.
Request timed out.
Request timed out.
Request timed out.
Request timed out.
Request timed out.
Request timed out.
Request timed out.
Request timed out.
Request timed out.
Request timed out.
Request timed out.
Request timed out.
Request timed out.
Request timed out.
Reply from 192.168.1.1: bytes=32 time<1ms TTL=64
Reply from 192.168.1.1: bytes=32 time<1ms TTL=64
Reply from 192.168.1.1: bytes=32 time<1ms TTL=64
Reply from 192.168.1.1: bytes=32 time<1ms TTL=64
```

You will see that the client is automatically getting a response now. Because you blocked the firewall, the firewall rules no longer apply. And the traffic is now being allowed freely. That is because there are no filters in place and the pfSense server is only acting as a router and not a firewall.

11. Now let's go back and uncheck the **Disable all packet filtering** option, and click the **Save** button. The pfSense server will again start acting as a firewall. This is because there are no other firewall rules defined. You can again go back and check the Command Prompt window on the client server, as shown in the following:

You will see that it has lost the connection again. So, this is how pfSense works as a router and can be enabled to act like a firewall, as well.

Firewall rules in pfSense

Now let's walk through the process of creating some firewall rules for the **LAN1** internal network segment:

1. Let's head back to the pfSense **Dashboard**. Click **Firewall**, and click **Rules**.

   In the following screenshot, you can see there is only one rule implemented for **LAN1**:

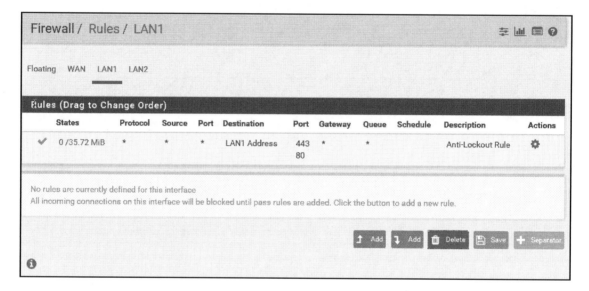

2. To add a new rule, you could use the **Add** buttons at the bottom. Notice that there are two **Add** buttons available here. The first one adds a rule to the top of the list while the second **Add** icon adds a rule to the end of the list. As we mentioned earlier, pfSense evaluates firewall rules in sequential order. pfSense starts to evaluate each firewall rule and stops at the first match. So, the order of these rules is extremely important.

3. Let's go ahead and create a new firewall rule at the top of the list. Click the first **Add** button:

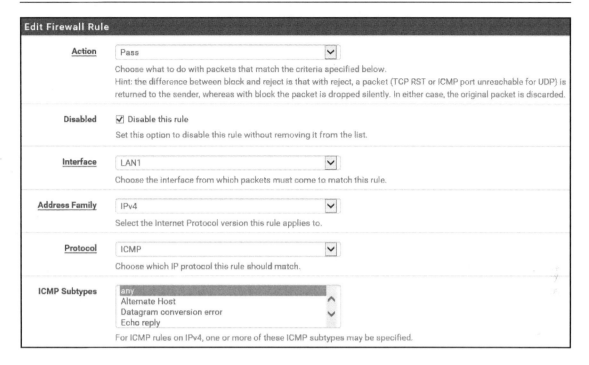

Now here you can add or edit a firewall rule. Let's review these options:

- The first option is **Action**, which defines whether pfSense should **Pass, Block**, or **Reject** network packets if they match this rule. If **Action** is set to **Pass**, then pfSense will allow that network packet to go through. If it's set to **Block**, it will block the network quietly. With **Reject**, it'll block the traffic, but it'll also send a rejection acknowledgment back to the client. In fact, a TCP RST or ICMP port unreachable by UDP is returned to the sender.
- Next is **Disabled;** if checked, this rule will be disabled and will not be evaluated by pfSense. It is a good practice to disable these rules while you're creating or editing them, so that the ongoing network traffic is not affected by the work-in-progress rules. So, let's check this box to disable this firewall rule. We'll re-enable it later when everything has been configured properly.
- Next is the network **Interface**, to which you want to attach this firewall rule. In this case, let's pick **LAN1**.
- Next is **Address Family**, which determines whether this firewall rule will apply to **IPv4** traffic or **IPv6** traffic.

- Next is a **Protocol**. Let's set **Protocol** to **ICMP**. And let's set **ICMP Subtypes** to **any**.
- Set the **Source** to **LAN1 net**. This refers to the LAN network, whereas the **LAN1 address** option refers to the single IP address. So with this setting, this rule will apply to any traffic originating from the **LAN1** network.

4. Set **Destination** to any. And then click **Save**.
5. Let's create another rule. Click the first **Add** button again. Tick the **Disable this rule** checkbox. Set **Protocol** as **TCP/UDP**. And set the **Source** as **LAN1 net**. Click the **Display Advanced** button to reveal the port range. Set the **Source Port Range** to **HTTP(80)**. And click **Save**:

This port range will allow HTTP traffic on port 80 from any source device on the **LAN1** network to any destination.

Okay, now back in the firewall rule listing page; you will observe that since we clicked the first **Add** button, which adds the rules at the top of the list, the second rule was added to the top of the list. Of course, pfSense is smart enough to not add any rule higher than the **Anti-Lock Out Rule**, because it needs to have precedence over all other rules. But if you had clicked the second **Add** item, the rule would have been added to the end of the list.

6. Let's try to add a rule to the end of the list now. Click the second **Add** button. Select the **Disabled by default** checkbox. Set the protocol to **TCP/UDP**. Now change the source to **LAN1 net**. Set the **Source port range** to **FTP(21)**. And then click **Save**:

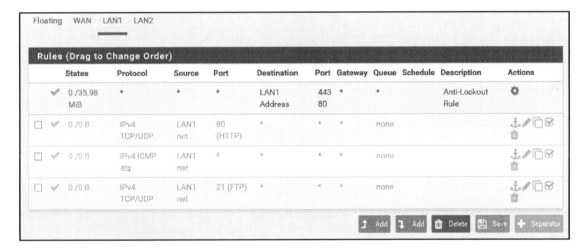

As you can see, the new FTP rule was added to the end of the list. That was a walk-through of how you can set up firewall rules in pfSense. These were just simple rules.

7. Let's perform some cleanup and delete these rules. And we will start with a clean slate in subsequent examples.
8. Click on the bin icon to delete these rules.
9. Click the **Apply Changes** button after deleting them.
10. Click on **Monitor** changes. And you can see that the changes have been saved and reloaded. Almost like the Matrix, but better!

Firewall rules for internal LAN networks

Now that you understand how to create, edit, and delete firewall rules, let's go ahead and create some meaningful firewall rules for LAN1.

In the previous example, we added some firewall rules and cleaned them up. Now there are no rules, allowing any type of traffic on LAN1. Let's confirm that by switching to the Windows 7 machine:

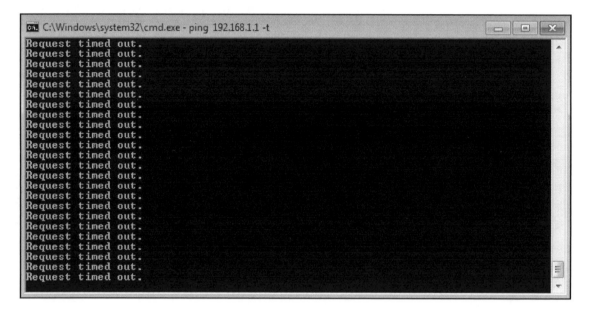

As you can see, `ping` requests are getting blocked here. Now let's go ahead and add a new firewall rule to allow LAN1 for ICMP, which in turn should allow these `ping` requests to go through.

Generally, it is always good to create rules in ascending order:

1. Click the first **Add** button. Make sure the **Action** is **Pass**. Also let's not check the **Disable these rules** option, because we intend to use them to pass the traffic through.
2. Set **Protocol** to **ICMP**.
3. Select **Source** as **LAN1 net** and the **Destination** as **any**.
4. Click **Save**. And then click **Apply Changes**. Click the **Monitor** link, and wait until the screen is refreshed.

5. Now go back to the client machine, and you can see that as soon as the configuration was saved, the ICMP protocol was allowed by pfSense because of the newly set rule:

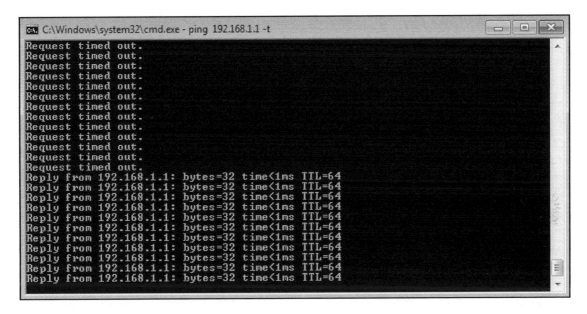

6. Let's go back and add a few more rules for different protocols.
7. Click the **Add** button. Make sure the **Action** is **Pass**, and the rule is not **Disabled**.
8. Set the **Protocol** to **TCP/UDP**, the **Source** to **LAN1 net**, and the **Source port range** to **DNS (53)**. And click **Save**.
9. Again, click the **Add** button.
10. Change the **Protocol** to **TCP/UDP**, the **Source** to **LAN1 net**, and the **Source port range** to **HTTP(80)**. And then click **Save**. What you're adding now are some industry standard rules that are primarily always allowed for someone to use the network and internet effectively.
11. Click the **Add** button. Change the **Protocol** to **TCP/UDP**. Set the **Source** to **LAN1 net**. Click **Display Advanced**.
12. Set the **Source port range** as **HTTPS(443)**. And then click **Save**.

13. Click the **Add** button again. As you may notice, we have a pattern going. Keep the same settings as the previous rule. Since we're creating rules for mail servers, you can change the **Source port range** based on your requirements. Different types of mail servers work on different network ports. For instance, if you have an IMAP mail server, you will choose port 143, or; for POP3 or POP3/S, you will set port 110 or 995, respectively. Or if you want to enable the SSH protocol, you can select port 22 here. Let's get back to the **LAN1** firewall rule listing page:

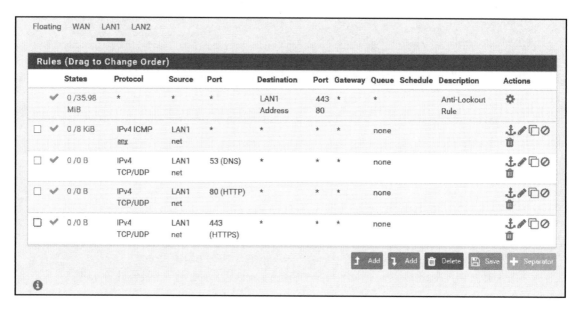

You can see we have four rules listed here, besides the **Anti-Lockout Rule**. So, this is how you create firewall rules in pfSense.

Setting up firewall rules for LAN2

You've seen how to configure firewall rules for **LAN1**. Now let's set up some firewall rules for **LAN2**:

1. Here, on the firewall rule listing page, click the **LAN2** tab. The basic process of creating rules here is the same as **LAN1**.
2. Click the **Add** button. You need to click the second **Add** button this time to add the rules at the bottom of the list. Anyway, let's make sure the **Action** is **Pass** and this rule is not **Disabled.**
3. Change the **Protocol** to **ICMP** and the **Source** to **LAN2 net**. Click **Save**.
4. Click the **Add** button again.

5. Set the **Protocol** to **TCP/UDP**, the **Source** to **LAN2 net**, and the **Source port range** to **DNS(53)**. And click **Save**:

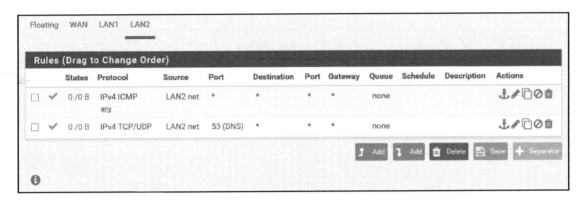

This is how you can create multiple rules on different LANs. Once you have created rules in both **LAN1** and **LAN2** based on your specific requirements, you need to add a rule to both LAN segments to ensure that **LAN1** or **LAN2** cannot interact with each other. If you recall, earlier we explained how **LAN1** must be isolated from **LAN2**, which is effectively the DMZ LAN network in this setup. Since pfSense is a router, some network packets may be transferred from one LAN to the other. But you can configure firewalls in place to avoid such packet transfers.

6. Let's add a rule for **LAN1** first. Click the **LAN1** tab. Click the **Add** button.
7. Set **Action** as **Reject**, and **Interface** as **LAN1**.
8. Set the **Protocol** to **TCP/UDP**. Set the **Source** to **LAN1 net** and **Destination** to **LAN2 net**. Then click the **Save** button:

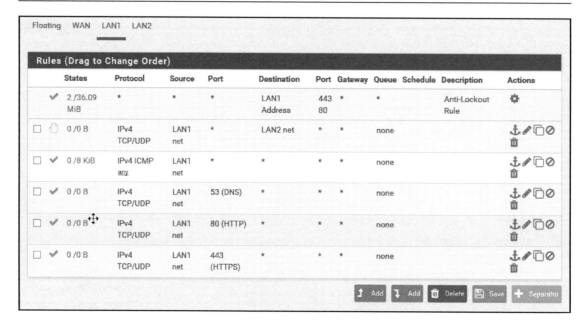

This rule has been set to basically reject all packets from the **Source LAN1** to **Destination LAN2**. All **TCP/UDP** originating from **LAN1** and destined for **LAN2** has now been blocked. So, the **LAN1** network cannot communicate with **LAN2**. And one of the most important things is that this rejection rule is at the top of the list. You must put all restrictive rules at the top, so that they get evaluated first, and sensitive traffic is blocked diligently.

9. Repeat the same steps for **LAN2**.
10. Click the **LAN2** tab. Click the first **Add** button.
11. Set **Action** as **Reject** and **Interface** as **LAN2**. Set the **Protocol** to **any**. Set the **Source** to **LAN2 net**, and **Destination** to **LAN1 net**.
12. Setting the **Protocol** to **any** is even more restrictive, because it will reject all traffic originating from **LAN2**, not just TCP or UDP traffic. So, as you can see, you have a tremendous amount of control over how to tweak your firewall rules to suit your specific needs for your network.
13. Let's click the **Save** button:

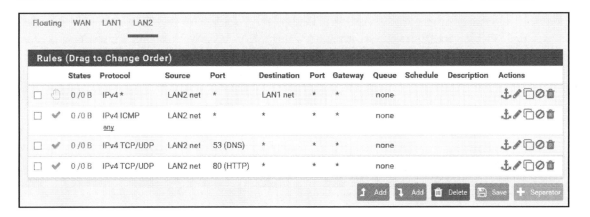

Once again, this rejection rule is on the top of the list for **LAN2** rules. Now all packets from source **LAN2** to destination **LAN1** will be rejected.

14. Click the **Apply Changes** button. Click **Monitor**, and wait for the **Done** notification. So, go back and refresh the page.

15. Let's go ahead and change the **Protocol** to **any** for the first rule for **LAN1** as well.

16. Go to the **LAN1** tab. Click the **Edit** icon for this rule. Set **Protocol** to **any**, and click **Save**.

Managing firewall rules

You have configured firewall rules for LAN1 and LAN2. Now, let's see how you can manage these rules. Now that you have created many rules for the firewall, you need to understand how to manage all of these rules efficiently and effectively.

If you want to add a new rule that is very similar to an existing rule, you can copy the existing rule.

1. Click the **LAN2** tab and try to create some new rules by copying existing rules. Here, we have only created ICMP and DNS rules. Let's create some more standard rules.

2. Click the copy icon under **Actions** for the **DNS (53)** rule. You can now make modifications to the rule as required. All the fields are copied from the original rule. For this instance, let's change the **Source port range** to **HTTP(80)** and leave the other fields as they are.

3. Click the **Save** button. And this is the quickest way to create new rules using existing rules.

4. Another option in the **Actions** panel is the **Disable** option. Let's say you want to disable the **Reject** rule so that **LAN1** and **LAN2** can communicate with each other. Just click the Disable icon. Click **Apply Changes**. This **Disable** button is a toggle button, by the way. You can re-enable the rule by clicking on this icon again. Similarly, go to **LAN1**. Do the same with one of the rule. Click **Apply Changes**.

Now both LAN segments can communicate with each other. You also have the option to move and change the order of the rules. So, just click the **Move** icon and drag the rule to the desired position. Finally, you can click the **Delete** icon to delete a rule.

5. Let's click the **Delete** icon for the **HTTPS 443** port rule:

And then click **OK**. Click **Apply Changes**. And you are done. Make sure you click the **Apply Changes** button after configuring these firewall rules.

Summary

Let's recap some of the key points covered in this chapter. You learned all about what firewalls are, their key functions, and importance. Next, you learned all about configuring pfSense as a firewall. You also learned how to set up firewall rules for multiple LANs, as well as how to manage these firewall rules using pfSense.

In the next chapter, you will learn about the load balancing and failover functionality provided by pfSense to work with multiple WAN connections.

3

pfSense as a Failover and Load Balancer

In the previous chapter, you learned about the firewall features supported by pfSense. You enabled the firewall and set up various rules to control the traffic flow within your network. In this chapter, you will learn how to configure pfSense to work with multiple WAN connections. You will also configure pfSense to failover and load balance the traffic across these WAN connections.

Here are some of the key learning objectives of this chapter:

- You will learn all about load balancing and failover processes across multiple WAN connections, and how to tie this in with pfSense
- You'll go through a series of demonstrations that will give you practical insight into configuring pfSense as a load balancer as well as a failover
- You will learn how to verify pfSense as a load balancer and as a failover

So, let's get started. To start with, let's understand what load balancing and failover are, and how they tie in with pfSense.

Load balancing and failover

Load balancing is a function used to divide the amount of work that a computer or a network has to do to accomplish a given task. In the case of pfSense, you can implement multiple ISP WAN connections and you can load balance your traffic between these connections. This means that when a device on the internal network makes a request to an external resource on a per-connection basis, pfSense can route the request over each WAN in a round-robin manner. If any gateway on the same tier goes down, it is removed from use and the other gateways on the tier continue to operate normally. Within the context of pfSense, a gateway is a system through which pfSense can reach the internet or another network.

Failover is basically the ability of a machine or a computer system to transfer an operation from a failed component to an alternative backup component without interrupting operations or process flow. When two gateways are on different tiers, the lower-tier gateway is preferred. If a lower-tier gateway goes down, it is removed from use and the next highest tier gateway is used. Let's understand these scenarios in more detail from the use case diagram shown here:

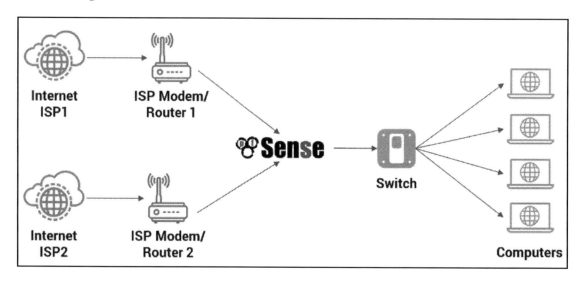

This diagram represents a typical pfSense setup to explain failover and load balancing. Let's first look at all of the components involved here. The first cloud represents the **Internet** connection or **ISP1**. There's also another cloud that serves as a second **Internet** connection or **ISP2**. So, these are basically two different ISPs, and each of them connects to two routers, **Router 1** and **Router 2**. Next, you can see that both routers are connected to the pfSense firewall. This leads to a **Switch**, which then leads to the different endpoints or hosts. So, in a nutshell, this diagram has two WAN ports connecting both **ISP1** and **ISP2** modems or routers to pfSense. It also has a single LAN port connecting to a switch and thereby connecting to the internal LAN network to the pfSense server.

First, let's discuss the failover scenario. Let's say you start off routing all the traffic to **ISP1**. Everything is working perfectly, until one fine and dandy day, **ISP1** experiences some technical hurdles and it goes down. If you did not have pfSense monitoring **ISP1**, you would have a few choices to deal with in this situation. You could either manually switch over to **ISP2** if you have one, or wait for **ISP1** to fix its technical problems. Obviously, both of these are less than desirable solutions. This is where pfSense's multi WAN support comes in. If you configure pfSense to work with multiple WAN connections and implement failover and/or load balancing, then the failover in these extreme cases is transparent to the internal LAN users. In this case, as soon as pfSense detects that **ISP1** is down, the traffic will be automatically redirected to **ISP2**:

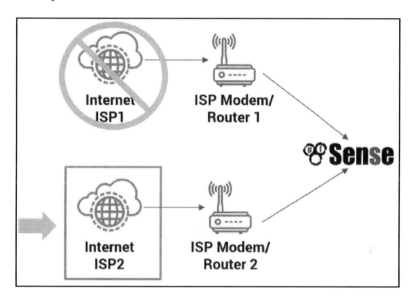

In this scenario, we can say that a proper failover has been configured. If **ISP2** is only used for failover, then pfSense will wait until **ISP1** is back up and running. When everything's returned back to normal, pfSense will start routing the traffic through **ISP1** again. So, this may be considered an **active-passive failover**.

The second scenario is about load balancing across multiple connections, even in non-exceptional cases. Let's say you have two ISP connections, but they're not the same in terms of their bandwidth offering, quality, and consistency of connectivity:

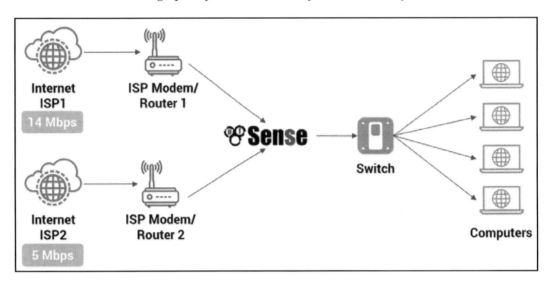

ISP1 is a premium provider that offers a bandwidth of **14** megabits per second and a more robust connection, while **ISP2** provides a bandwidth of **5** megabits per second. Now, instead of wasting the bandwidth provided by the second ISP, you could configure pfSense to load balance the traffic across both connections and utilize both ISPs to their maximum advantage. Once again, pfSense is extremely flexible in terms of how you implement this load balancing. You could choose to combine the bandwidth from both connections and use both these ISPs simultaneously, and the load will be distributed among both ISPs. You could also route the traffic across these two ISPs based on certain criteria. For instance, you could configure pfSense to route all HTTP traffic via **ISP1**, whereas all FTP traffic could be routed to **ISP2**. A more usual case is that voice and video communication traffic is generally routed via a more robust and bigger ISP, whereas regular email and web traffic is routed via the cheaper alternative ISP. An added advantage of load balancing is that the failover works without any additional configuration. If **ISP1** is down, all the traffic will be forwarded to **ISP2**, and vice versa, so that the entire network does not experience any downtime. This may be considered **active-active load balancing**.

Now, let's look at the load balancing scenario:

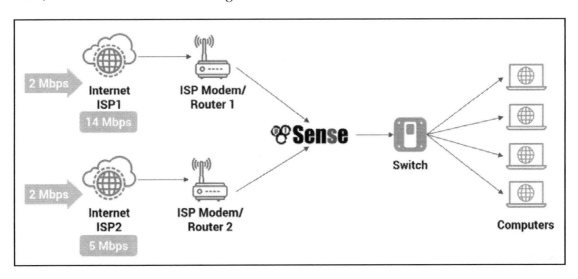

In this scenario, consider that **ISP1** has a bandwidth of **14** megabits per second, while **ISP2** has a bandwidth of **5** megabits per second. Now, if the internet network is using **2 Mbps**, it will use both of these ISPs simultaneously and the load will be distributed among both ISPs based on certain criteria. This scenario demonstrates the conditions required for pfSense to work as a load balancer, and it also shows that it has been configured properly. If **ISP1** is down, all the traffic will be forwarded to **ISP2**, and vice versa, so that the entire network does not experience downtime.

Load balancing and failover across multiple WAN connections

Now, let's go ahead and configure pfSense to act as a load balancer across multiple WAN connections:

1. Let's switch to the pfSense server. Here we are at the command-line dashboard for pfSense:

```
Enter an option: restart

\VirtualBox Virtual Machine - Netgate Device ID: 9e6eeb2755c53e6da6b9

*** Welcome to pfSense 2.4.3-RELEASE (amd64) on pfSense ***

 WAN (wan)         -> em0         -> v4/DHCP4: 10.0.2.15/24
 LAN1 (lan)        -> em1         -> v4: 192.168.1.1/24
 WAN2 (opt1)       -> em2         -> v4/DHCP4: 192.168.1.103/24

 0) Logout (SSH only)                9) pfTop
 1) Assign Interfaces               10) Filter Logs
 2) Set interface(s) IP address     11) Restart webConfigurator
 3) Reset webConfigurator password  12) PHP shell + pfSense tools
 4) Reset to factory defaults       13) Update from console
 5) Reboot system                   14) Enable Secure Shell (sshd)
 6) Halt system                     15) Restore recent configuration
 7) Ping host                       16) Restart PHP-FPM
 8) Shell

Enter an option: █
```

You can see here that we have configured two WAN connections. The first WAN interface is em0 and the WAN2 interface is em2. Both of them have different IPs. The LAN1 interface is em1. Basically, the third network interface was renamed from LAN2 to WAN2, and instead of connecting it to an internal switch, the third network interface was connected to a new ISP.

2. Let's use the Windows 2012 R2 machine to access the WebGUI console.

Additionally, you can also use the Windows 7 client system to test the connectivity.

3. Let's move on to the configuration process for load balancing and also for failover.

4. Open the WebGUI of pfSense from Windows Server 2012 R2. If you remember, the pfSense server IP address is `192.168.1.1`.

5. Navigate to that IP address and enter the login details in the pfSense console and click the **Login** button.

   The pfSense **Dashboard** is displayed and lists all the details:

6. You can see three interfaces, one LAN and two WAN ports. **WAN** has a public IP address, while **LAN1** has a private IP address.

7. Click on the **Interfaces** tab and click **WAN.** Change the name to WAN1 for consistency. Click **Save.**

8. Click **Apply Changes** and go back to the **Dashboard.**

Now, the **Interfaces** are named consistently:

Interfaces			
⬢ WAN1	⬆	1000baseT <full-duplex>	10.0.2.15
⬢ LAN1	⬆	1000baseT <full-duplex>	192.168.1.1
⬢ WAN2	⬆	1000baseT <full-duplex>	192.168.1.103

It is much easier to discern the purpose of each of these **Interfaces** based on the names. It is good practice to follow a consistent naming scheme for your networking components.

Configuring Gateway Groups

To configure pfSense as a load balancer or failover, you first need to create a **Gateway Group**. Let's do that now.

Before you start, let's first check if the client system has internet connectivity or not. Let's switch to the Windows 7 client system:

1. Open a browser window and navigate to a site, say google.com, and check the connectivity. You can also check this by opening the Command Prompt. Execute the ping google.com -t command:

```
C:\Users\packt>ping google.com -t

Pinging google.com [216.58.220.174] with 32 bytes of data:
Reply from 216.58.220.174: bytes=32 time=54ms TTL=52
Reply from 216.58.220.174: bytes=32 time=43ms TTL=52
Reply from 216.58.220.174: bytes=32 time=50ms TTL=52
Reply from 216.58.220.174: bytes=32 time=41ms TTL=52
Reply from 216.58.220.174: bytes=32 time=44ms TTL=52
Reply from 216.58.220.174: bytes=32 time=40ms TTL=52
Reply from 216.58.220.174: bytes=32 time=40ms TTL=52
Reply from 216.58.220.174: bytes=32 time=40ms TTL=52
Reply from 216.58.220.174: bytes=32 time=41ms TTL=52
Reply from 216.58.220.174: bytes=32 time=40ms TTL=52
Reply from 216.58.220.174: bytes=32 time=39ms TTL=52
Reply from 216.58.220.174: bytes=32 time=40ms TTL=52
```

As you can see, the `ping` command is working fine.

2. Now that you have verified the connectivity on the client machine, let's go back to the pfSense server.

3. Go to **System** tab and click **Routing:**

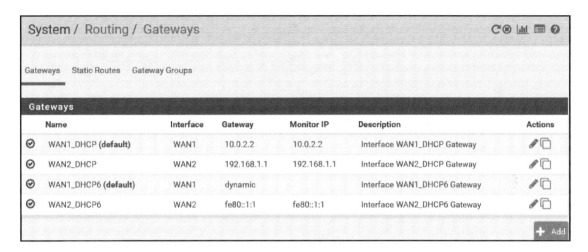

In the **Gateways** tab, you can see that there are two gateways—**WAN1** and **WAN2**, which are defined here. **WAN1** is the default gateway. There is still another gateway for both, but it is for **DHCP6**, which is related to the IPv6 IP addresses. For now, let's just focus on the IPv4 IP network.

As mentioned earlier, a pfSense gateway is a system through which pfSense can reach the internet or another network.

4. Let's switch to the **Gateway Groups** tab:

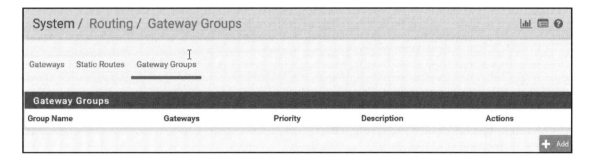

As you can see, currently, this pfSense server does not have any **Gateway Groups** defined. Let's take care of that now.

5. Click the **Add** button to create a new **Gateway Group**. You will be redirected to this window:

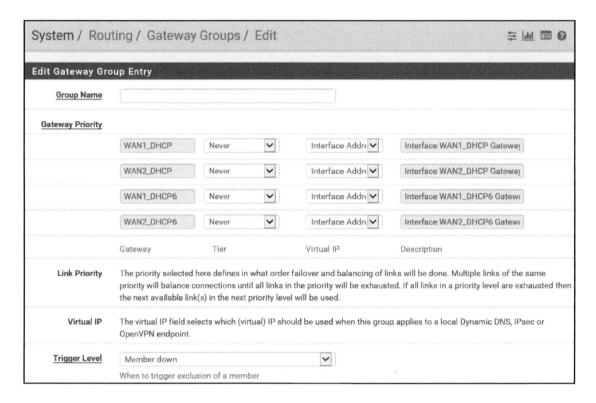

6. You will now create a **Gateway Group** by adding the two gateways, **WAN1** and **WAN2**. A Gateway Group is just a simple way to group together gateways to act in a coordinated fashion. These gateway groups can perform load balancing, failover, or a mixture of the two. As you may have guessed, this is the core component that provides the load balancing and failover capabilities to pfSense.

7. Let's name the new **Gateway Group** `WAN_Group`. Change the **Gateway Priority** of **WAN1_DHCP** to `Tier 1`. Do the same with **WAN2_DHCP**:

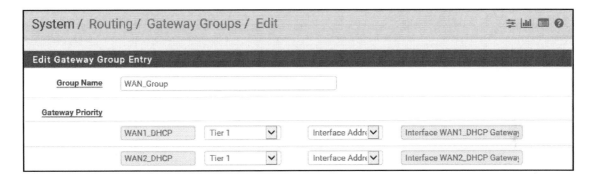

In a pfSense **Gateway Group**, each gateway is assigned to a tier to determine when and how it is used. The lower tier numbers are preferred over the higher tier numbers. If any two gateways are on the same tier, then those gateways will load balance. If they're on different tiers, they will perform failover, preferring the lower tier. If the tier is set to **Never**, then the **Gateway** is not considered part of this group.

8. Click **Save** and the **Gateway** configuration will have been change. The changes must be applied to take effect. So, click **Apply Changes** and click the **Gateways** tab.

You already have **Gateway WAN1** as the default, which means pfSense will route all outgoing traffic via **WAN1**. But the intent here is to route all the traffic through the load balanced Gateway Group you just created. To change this, you need to configure a new firewall rule:

1. Click the **Firewall** tab from the top toolbar and click **Rules**.
2. Click the **LAN1** tab. Here, you will create a new rule, like we did in the previous chapter.
3. Click the first **Add** button.

Make sure you click the first **Add** button so that the rule is created at the top of the list.

On clicking the **Add** button, you will be redirected to the **Rules / Edit** window.

4. Let's define this rule now. Set the **Action** as **Pass**:

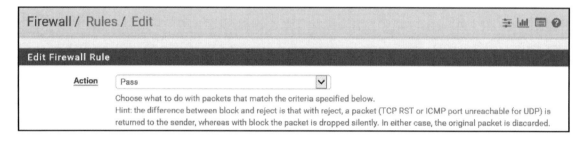

5. Change the **Source** to **LAN1 net**, and keep the **Destination** as **any**:

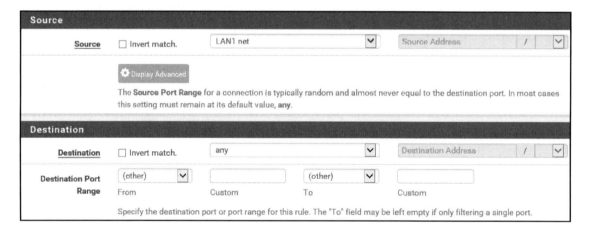

6. You can click the **Display Advanced** button under **Extra Options** to reveal some other settings for this firewall rule.

7. Scroll down and find a setting for **Gateway**. Change it to **WAN_Group**:

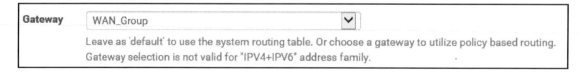

8. Click **Save**. Click **Apply Changes** and refresh. You can see that the rules have been reloaded in the **Dashboard**:

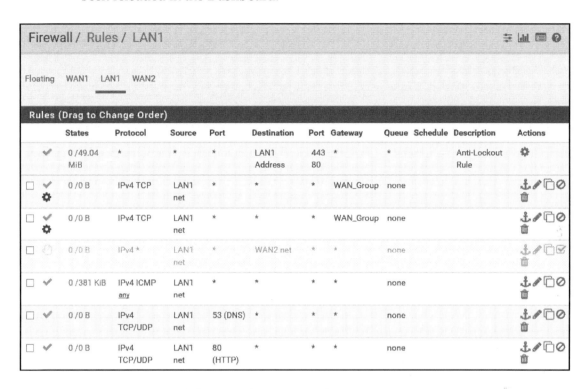

In this example, you walked through the process of setting up a Gateway Group and associating it with a firewall rule. Effectively, this sets up this pfSense server to start load balancing the traffic across multiple WAN connections transparently.

Verifying load balancing across WAN connections

Now, let's verify this setup and confirm that pfSense is able to load balance the traffic across multiple WAN connections. Let's head back to the pfSense WebGUI dashboard:

1. Click on the **Status** tab and then select **Gateways**. Click the **Gateway Groups** tab:

You can see that the components of this Gateway Group are online. Since this is a load balance group, as long as a single gateway is online, this Gateway Group will be able to serve traffic to the end users. Let's switch to the client machine.

2. In the Command Prompt window, let's execute the `ping google.com -t` command:

```
C:\Users\packt>ping google.com -t

Pinging google.com [216.58.220.174] with 32 bytes of data:
Reply from 216.58.220.174: bytes=32 time=54ms TTL=52
Reply from 216.58.220.174: bytes=32 time=43ms TTL=52
Reply from 216.58.220.174: bytes=32 time=50ms TTL=52
Reply from 216.58.220.174: bytes=32 time=41ms TTL=52
Reply from 216.58.220.174: bytes=32 time=44ms TTL=52
Reply from 216.58.220.174: bytes=32 time=40ms TTL=52
Reply from 216.58.220.174: bytes=32 time=40ms TTL=52
Reply from 216.58.220.174: bytes=32 time=40ms TTL=52
Reply from 216.58.220.174: bytes=32 time=41ms TTL=52
Reply from 216.58.220.174: bytes=32 time=40ms TTL=52
Reply from 216.58.220.174: bytes=32 time=39ms TTL=52
Reply from 216.58.220.174: bytes=32 time=40ms TTL=52
```

And as you can see, it is still able to `ping` the remote machine, and it is getting a valid response back. So basically, this external traffic is being routed via the pfSense server in a load balanced fashion.

3. Press *Ctrl + C* to stop the `ping` command. Let's go back to the WebGUI.

4. Now, let's try to simulate a situation where one of the WAN connections experiences an outage. To do that, you can just disable the WAN network interface. To configure this, click the **Interfaces** tab on the top toolbar, and click **WAN1**.

5. Uncheck the **Enable interface** checkbox. This will effectively disable the WAN interface and no traffic will pass through this interface.

6. Scroll down and click **Save**. Click **Apply Changes**.

Now, one of your interfaces is down. Go to the client machine and test the connectivity as we did previously with the `ping` command.

You will notice that even though the WAN connection is down, you're still getting a valid response. That is because pfSense has already realized that the WAN1 connection is down, so it needs to route all the traffic via WAN2.

Now, let's go back to WebGUI. Enable the interface by selecting the **Enable interface** checkbox. Click **Save** and click **Apply Changes**. You will see the client machine still getting responses. This is how pfSense load balancing works across multiple WAN connections.

Failover across multiple WAN connections

Now, pfSense has been configured for load balancing and implicit failover. Let's proceed and verify this configuration further.

Let's take the verification one step further. Instead of disabling a WAN connection, let's try to disable each of the gateways and observe the effects:

1. Click **System** tab on the toolbar and select **Routing**. Click the **Gateway Groups** tab:

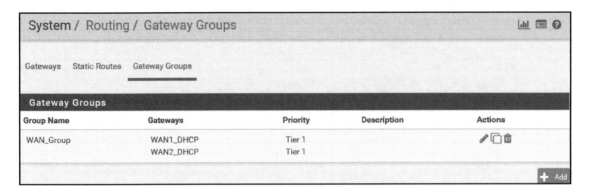

Both have the **Priority** set to **Tier 1**, which indicates that pfSense is currently working as a load balancer, which inherently also provides failover.

2. Click the **Gateways** tab and let's disable the first link, which is **WAN1-DHCP**:

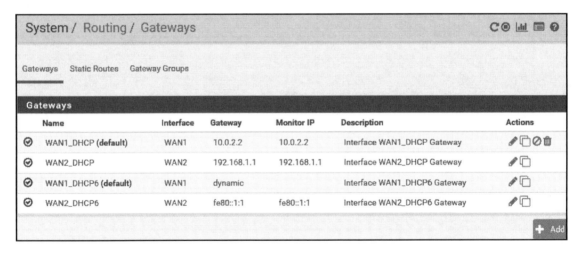

3. Click the **Edit** icon to its left. Scroll down to the field **Force State**. Select the **Mark Gateway as Down** checkbox:

Force state	☑ Mark Gateway as Down
	This will force this gateway to be considered down.

4. Click **Save**. Click **Apply Changes**. Go back to the client machine and see if it is getting a response. You will see that there isn't any drop in the connectivity as the traffic is being routed automatically through the second ISP, that is, the WAN2 interface.

5. Go back to the WebGUI. Click the **Edit** icon for the WAN1 interface. Deselect the **Mark Gateway as Down** checkbox, and click **Save**. Click **Apply Changes**.

6. Now, click the **Edit** icon for the second link, WAN2. Scroll down to the **Force State** field. Select the **Mark Gateway as Down** checkbox and click **Save**. Click **Apply Changes**.

7. Go back to the client machine and see if it is getting a response. You will see that there doesn't seem to be any drop in the connectivity.

So, this is how you can configure the pfSense server as a load balancer or failover across multiple WAN connections. In this case, both WAN connections were assigned to the same tier, but if you change the tiers of these gateways, say WAN1 is assigned to Tier 1 and WAN2 is assigned to Tier 2, then pfSense will behave strictly in a failover mode. The lower tier will be used first. If that fails, pfSense will automatically failover to the other WAN connection with the higher tier number.

Summary

Let's just quickly recap some of the key points that we have covered in this chapter. You learned all about the load balancing and failover features of pfSense. Next, you learned to configure pfSense as a load balancer and a failover mechanism across multiple WAN connections. Finally, you verified the failover and load balancing behavior of pfSense and its effect on the network traffic.

In the next chapter, you will learn about remote connectivity options that are available in pfSense.

4

Remote Connectivity with pfSense and IPsec

Welcome to this chapter on setting up remote connectivity with pfSense and IPsec VPN Tunnel. In the last chapter, you learned how you could configure pfSense as a load balancing router across multiple WANs. You also learned how to leverage this functionality and implement a failover mechanism for your ISP connections. In this chapter, you will learn about IPsec, its features, and how it is used. You'll also learn how to configure an IPsec VPN tunnel in the pfSense server.

Here are some of the key topics of this chapter:

- IPsec and its key features
- The different types of security association modes
- A series of demonstrations that will give you practical insight into configuring an IPsec tunnel on the pfSense server

So, what are we waiting for? Let's get going.

What is IPsec?

IPsec, also known as **Internet Protocol Security**, is a protocol suite that encrypts IP traffic before the packets are transferred from the source node to the destination. So, naturally, a question arises: what are packets? Well, let's see.

Packets are the basic unit of information in a network transmission. Networks that use TCP as their network protocol transfer data in IP packets. These IP packets have the source and destination address along with the data to be transferred. IPsec is a set of protocols that enable machines to establish mutual authentication between agents at the start of the IPsec session. They also help in the negotiation of cryptographic keys to use during the secure session. IPsec is a versatile suite of protocols and it supports multiple scenarios. IPsec can protect data flows between a pair of hosts (host-to-host), a pair of security gateways (network-to-network), or between a security gateway and a host (network-to-host). IPsec uses strong cryptography to protect communications over Internet Protocol networks or IP networks. IPsec supports network-level pure authentication, data origin authentication, data integrity, data confidentiality, encryption, and replay protection.

Transport mode

The IPsec protocols can be implemented in host-to-host transport mode, as well as in a network tunneling mode. In the transport mode, IPsec only encrypts the payload of the IP packet. No other part of the IP packet is tampered with. Since the IP header is neither modified nor encrypted, the network routing for each packet remains intact.

Tunnel mode

Under the tunnel IPsec mode, the entire IP packet is encrypted and authenticated. This encrypted IP packet is then encapsulated into a new IP packet with a new IP header. Basically, it encrypts the entire IP traffic before the transfer of packets.

 IPsec tunnel mode supports NAT traversal, and it is the default mode.

With tunnel mode, the entire original IP packet is protected by IPsec. This means that the IPsec wraps the original packet, encrypts it, adds a new IP header, and sends it to the other side of the VPN tunnel-IPsec peer.

IPsec features

IPsec is the most secure, commercially available method to connect network remote clients and sites. IPsec was designed to provide a secure and robust mechanism to transfer the IP packets privately across networks. IPsec has a number of features baked into the protocol, which makes it so secure and robust. An authentication mechanism inherent in the IPsec protocol verifies that the packet received is actually from the claimed sender. IPsec uses strong cryptography to assert and verify the integrity of data. This ensures that the contents of the packet did not change during transit. And, of course, with the help of encryption, IPsec ensures confidentiality. It conceals the message's content through encryption while it is in flight.

Security Association

Let's get familiar with another term, called **Security Association (SA)**. The concept of SA is fundamental to IPsec. An SA is a relationship between two or more entities, nodes, or devices on disparate networks that describes how these entities will use security services to communicate securely. IPsec provides many options for performing network encryption and authentication. In other words, an SA is a logical connection between two devices transferring data. It provides data protection for unidirectional traffic using defined IPsec protocols. An IPsec tunnel typically consists of a pair of unidirectional SAs, which together provide a protected full duplex data channel. The SAs allow a network administrator to control exactly what resources may communicate securely according to a security policy. You can set up multiple SAs to enable multiple secure VPNs. It can also define SAs within the VPN to support different departments and business partners.

IPsec VPN tunnel implementation

Let's look at an IPSec VPN tunnel implementation example:

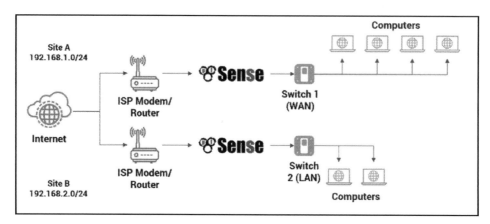

The cloud icon represents a public unsecured network, say the **Internet**. Let's say there are two remote office sites, **Site A** and **Site B**. This could be two branch offices of a company situated in different cities or even different countries. Both of these remote sites have their own independent ISP connections. They also have a local pfSense firewall implemented in remote locations. Similarly, they also have an internal LAN, consisting of various internal network devices. **Site A** has the internal IP address range of 192.168.1.0/24. **Site B** has the internal IP address range of 192.168.2.0/24. In this scenario, these two sites are protecting their local internet networks with an installation of pfSense. But what if these two sites need to connect to each other? Or all the branch offices need to connect to the main head office network? In these situations, you can implement a secure and persistent IPSec tunnel between these sites. This will enable a secure network data flow between the connected sites. For the end users within the internal networks on remote sites, the entire connected network, including the branch office, will appear as a single logical connected network. By implementing these IPSec VPN tunnels, it is possible to use IPsec to send internet traffic from **Site A** in a way that it appears to be coming from **Site B**, and vice versa.

Prerequisites

Now, let's review some of the prerequisites you need to take care of before setting up IPsec VPN tunnels in pfSense. When you are trying to establish IPsec tunnels between two networks, you must make sure that both locations are using non-overlapping LAN IP subnets. For example, if both sites are using 10.0.0.0/24 on the LAN segment, the IPsec site-to-site VPN will not work. This is not a limitation in pfSense; it's due to basic IP routing. If the pfSense server is not the default gateway on the LAN where it is installed, then some static routes must be added to the default gateway pointing the remote VPN subnet to the IP address on pfSense in the LAN subnet. You must have good communication with the administrator of the remote network so that you can coordinate the activities that are needed to set up the IPsec tunnel. There are a lot of settings that need to match on both sides of the tunnel, so, regular communication and cooperation with the remote administrator will be very, very helpful.

IPsec phases

IPsec tunnels are based on two components. Phase 1 of the IPsec protocol defines the remote peer and how the tunnel is authenticated. One or more Phase 2 entries of the IPsec protocol define how traffic is carried across the secure tunnel. It is very important to configure these two phases carefully. If the information is incorrect in either section, the tunnel will likely fail to successfully negotiate Phase 1 and/or Phase 2. You need to make sure that both VPN servers have exactly the same settings for all of the IPsec configuration fields, with only a few exceptions to that rule. For example, both sides will have different identifiers and remote gateways. The subnet definitions, timeouts, encryption settings, and so on all need to match.

Configuring IPsec tunnel

Now that you're familiar with the IPsec concepts, let's go ahead and implement a new IPsec tunnel in the pfSense server:

1. Login to pfSense by inputting credentials and go to the pfSense dashboard.
2. Now, let's go ahead and configure a new IPsec tunnel. Let's click **VPN** on the top toolbar, and click **IPsec**.

As you will see, right now there are no **IPsec** VPN tunnels configured here:

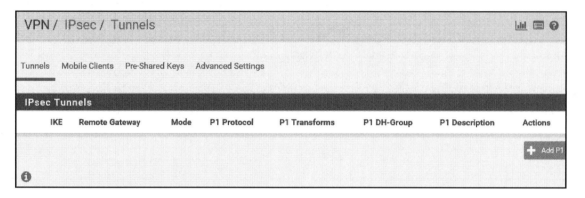

For this example, let's assume that this particular instance of pfSense is installed in Site A.

3. Under the **Tunnels** tab, click the **Add P1** button. P1 here refers to Phase 1. Ensure that the **Disabled** checkbox is not checked, otherwise the IPsec tunnel will not be enabled:

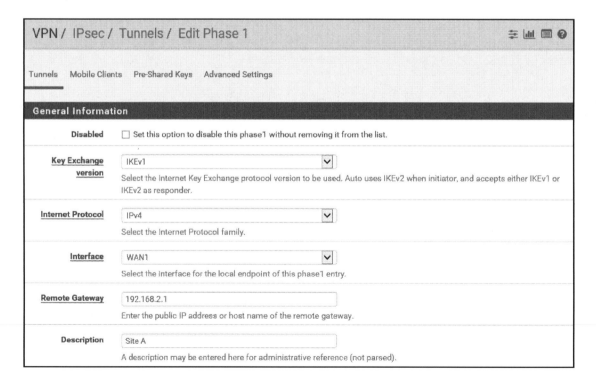

pfSense will suggest default values for most of these settings related to IPsec. The **Internet Protocol** for this IPsec tunnel is **IPv4**, which is what you want. The **Interface** is **WAN1**, which is also good. In the **Description** field, let's input `Site A`. In the **Remote Gateway** field, you need to enter the public IP address of the remote site, which is `192.168.2.1`.

This is the IP address for the remote pfSense or IPsec tunnel endpoint, to which **Site A** will be connected. In most cases, this should be the WAN IP of the remote system. A hostname may also be used in this field. In this case, let's enter `192.168.2.1`. This is the public IP address of Site B.

The next section deals with **Phase 1 Proposal** settings, which affect the authentication phase of the IPsec handshake:

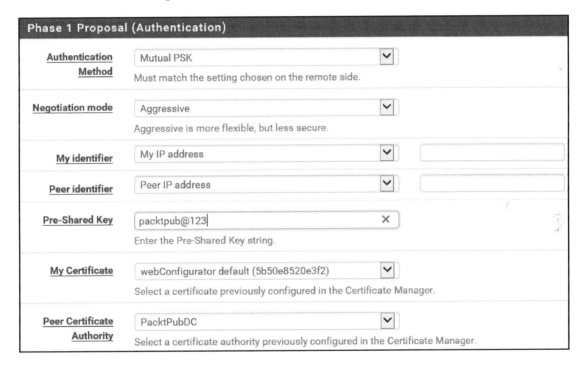

In the **Authentication Method** field, let's accept the default values of **Mutual PSK**. Here, you have to make sure that the method you choose matches the settings you chose on the remote site. **PSK** here stands for **Pre-Shared Key**. When PSK mode is used, the provided credentials will be in the form of a shared secret string. Let's change the **Negotiation mode** to **Aggressive**, since it is more flexible.

This is the type of authentication security scheme that will be used during the establishment of the secure IPsec tunnel. Aggressive negotiation mode is slightly less secure. It is far faster and will ensure that the VPN tunnel will rebuild itself quickly, and it probably won't timeout an application if the tunnel was down when the resource on the other end was requested.

For the identifier, let's accept the default values. **My identifier** identifies the current router to the remote router. It is best left as **My IP address,** and pfSense will fill it in as needed.

Peer identifier identifies the router on the remote site. It is best left as **Peer IP address** and pfSense will fill it in as needed.

The **Pre-Shared Key** is analogous to a password for the tunnel. As the name suggests, this key should be the same on both sides. The characters in this key string are case sensitive, and you can include special characters. You must make sure that this is a complex and long key to make sure it is secure. Since this only gets entered once on each side, there is no need to remember it. Let's enter `packtpub@123`.

For **Encryption Algorithm**, let's pick **AES**, because it is superior, faster, and more secure than other supported encryption algorithms:

Make sure that whatever algorithm you choose here matches the settings on the remote site as well. The **Hash** algorithm option is the hash used for the checksum. Let's change it to **SHA256** for better security.

In the **Advanced Options** section, make sure that the **NAT Traversal** is set to **Auto**. Keep all the other settings as they are and click the **Save** button:

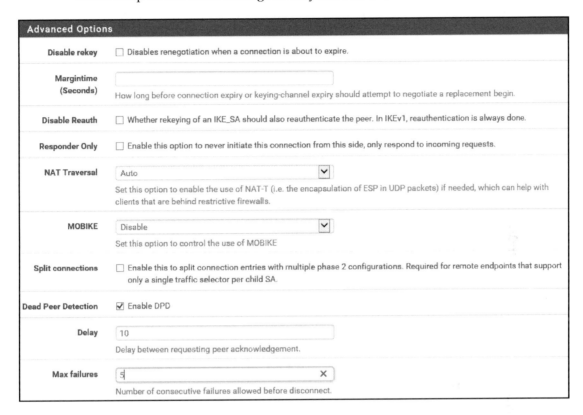

You have successfully configured Phase 1 of the IPsec VPN tunnel. Click **Apply Changes**.

4. Next, click the **Show Phase 2 Entries** button:

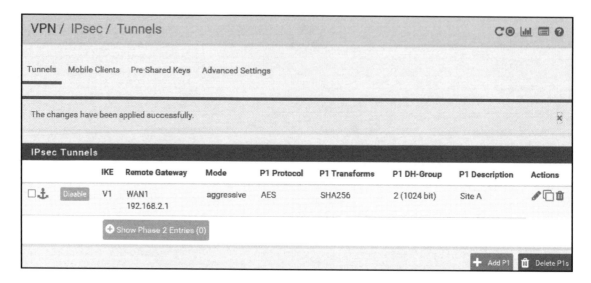

As you will see, there are currently no **Phase 2** entries for this IPsec tunnel:

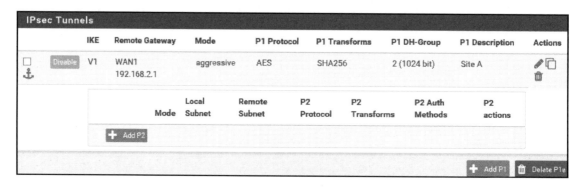

5. Click the **Add P2** button:

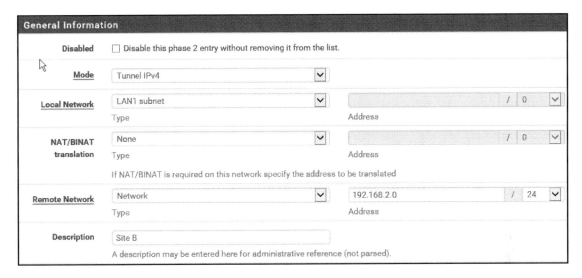

Once again, make sure that the **Disabled** checkbox is unchecked, and let's make sure that the **Mode** is set to **Tunnel IPv4**. The setting for **Local Network** defines which subnet or host can be accessed from the other side of the VPN tunnel. It is recommended that you set this to **LAN1 subnet**, which means that the entire LAN will be accessible from the remote network. So, let's change the **Local Network** to **LAN1 subnet**. This automatically selects the **LAN1 subnet** in the site. If you select **Address**, you can add the address manually.

Similarly, the **Remote Network** defines which subnet or host can be accessed through the secure IPsec tunnel. As mentioned previously, it is very important that these settings are set exactly like the other end's local subnet section. If not, Phase 2 of the VPN connection will fail, and traffic will not pass from one VPN segment to the other. In the **Remote Network** field, let's enter 192.168.2.0, and keep the subnet mask as **24**. In the **Description** field, enter **Site B**.

6. Now, under the **Phase 2 Proposal** section, you can define the settings that affect the encryption and handshake:

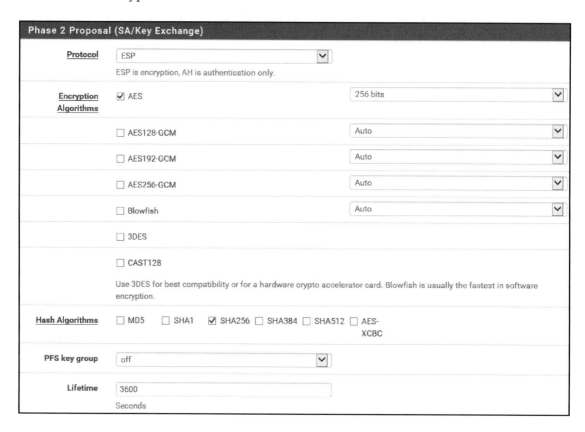

The **Encryption Algorithms** should be the same for Sites A and B. So, select **256 bits** in the **AES** drop-down list.

Similarly, for **Hash Algorithms**, select **SHA256**.

Leave the other settings as the default selections and click the **Save** button. Then, click on **Apply Changes:**

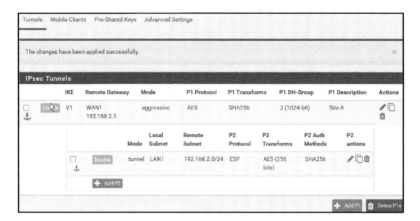

And this is how you configure Site A's IPsec VPN tunnel. The process to configure Site B's VPN tunnel is the same as what you did for Site A. The only difference will be in the local IP address. For Site B, it will be `192.168.2.0/24`, and the remote IP will be Site A's network address.

Configuring pfSense firewall rules

You've already set up the IPsec VPN tunnel, but pfSense will not allow any traffic through unless a firewall rule is established to pass it. So, let's look at the process of configuring a firewall rule to pass the IPsec traffic. Click on **Firewall**, and select **Rules:**

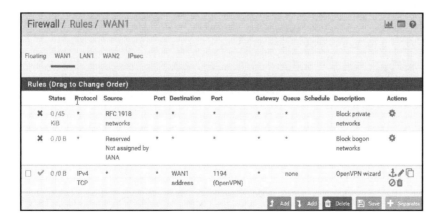

Notice that a new tab called **IPsec** is available here. Let's click the **IPsec** tab. You will see that there are no firewall rules defined here. So, click the first **Add** button to create a new rule:

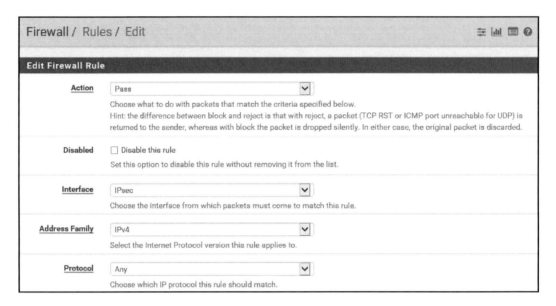

Make sure that the **Action** is set to **Pass**, the **Interface** is set to **IPsec**, and the **Address Family** is set to **IPv4**.

Also, change the **Protocol** to **Any** to allow for any type of traffic over the secure IPsec tunnel.

Accept all the default values for the rest of the settings and click the **Save** button. Then, click the **Apply Changes** button.

Once it's done, let's go back and refresh the page:

The **Firewall** rule has been established. The **IPsec** tunnel should now be operational. You should be able to `ping` from one site to the other.

However, computers on Site A are not yet connected to the internet. To do this, you need to configure a NAT rule for this IPsec tunnel. So, click **Firewall** and select **NAT**, and then click the **Outbound** tab:

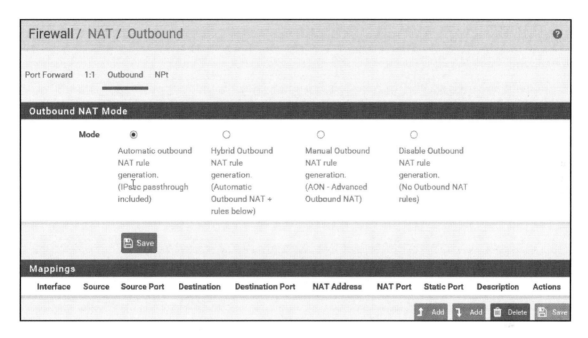

The default mode is **Automatic outbound NAT rule generation (IPsec passthrough included)**.

Click the **Save** button. Click the **Apply Changes** button. Now, go back and refresh the page. The changes have been applied.

Click the **Add** button to add a new rule. In the **Source** field, enter Site A's IP address, **192.168.1.0**, with a subnet mask of **24**:

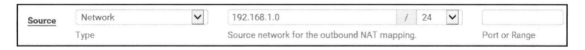

This is done because traffic will be generated from Site A.

In the **Description** field, enter **NAT for IPsec**:

Click the **Save** button. Click the **Apply Changes** button:

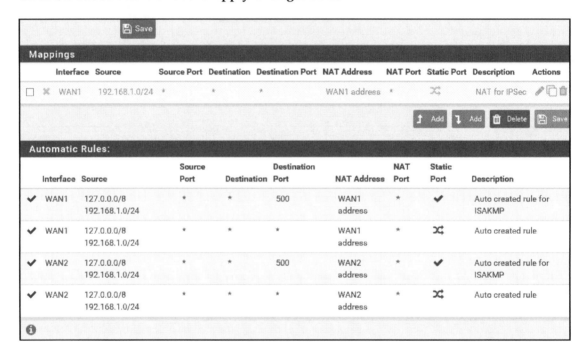

Now, you're all set. Both sites should have internet access. You can repeat these steps for Site B as well. Keep the settings and parameters the same for both sites.

Summary

Let's recap some of the key points covered in this chapter. You learned all about what IPsec is and its key features. You also learned about the different types of security association modes. Next, you learned how to configure an IPsec tunnel on pfSense for different sites. You also learned how to create firewall and NAT rules to allow traffic through the IPsec tunnels. In the final chapter, you will learn about a proxy server implementation called Squid proxy server.

5
Using pfSense as a Squid Proxy Server

In the previous chapter, you got familiar with the IPsec protocol, and you also learned how to implement IPsec tunnels on the pfSense platform. In this chapter, you will learn how to configure pfSense as a Squid proxy server. You will be integrating the Squid Proxy into pfSense, and then testing it using client access.

Here are some of the key learning objectives of this chapter:

- You will learn all about proxy servers, what they are, and their key features
- You'll also get an understanding of the advantages of a Squid proxy server
- You'll go through a series of demonstrations that will give you a practical insight into installing and configuring the Squid proxy server
- You will learn how to test the Squid proxy server in a client environment

Let's kick this module off by understanding what a proxy server is.

The proxy server

A **proxy server** is a hardware or a software system that acts as an intermediary between an endpoint device and another server, from which a user or client is requesting a service. The proxy server can exist on the same machine as a firewall server. It can also be on a separate server that forwards requests through the firewall. A proxy server's cache can serve all users. This is one of its key advantages. If one or more internet sites are frequently requested, these are likely to be in the proxy's cache. This improves user response time. It also helps relieve the pressure on a common shared network. Since the proxy server caches the content, it can save on the precious bandwidth consumption. A proxy server can also log its interactions, which can be helpful for troubleshooting. Let's have a look at a simple example to understand how proxy servers work:

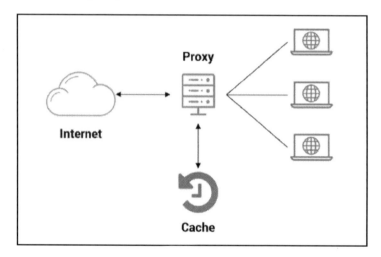

When a **Proxy** server receives a request for an internet resource, such as a web page, it looks in its local **Cache** of pages. If the **Proxy** server finds the requested resource in its **Cache**, then it returns it to the original requester without needing to forward the request to the remote server. If the requested resource is not in the **Cache**, the **Proxy** server acts as a client on behalf of the user. The **Proxy** server uses one of its IP addresses to request the page from the server on the internet. When the requested resource is returned, the **Proxy** server relates it to the original request, and forwards it on to the user.

Proxy servers can serve multiple purposes. In an enterprise, a proxy server is primarily used to facilitate security, administrative control, caching services, and so on. In a personal computing context, proxy servers are used to enable user privacy and anonymous surfing. Proxy servers can also be used for the opposite purpose – to monitor traffic and undermine user privacy. To the user, the proxy server is almost invisible. All internet requests and return responses appear to be direct with the addressed internet server. That being said, the user must specify the proxy server's IP address as a configuration option to the browser or other protocol programs. Okay, now you know what a proxy server is. Next, let's discuss what exactly the Squid proxy server is.

The Squid proxy server

Squid is a caching and forwarding web proxy. Squid is quite versatile and can serve multiple purposes, from speeding up a web server by caching repeated requests, to caching web, DNS, and other computer network lookups for a group of people sharing network resources, to aiding security by filtering traffic. Although primarily used for HTTP and FTP, Squid includes limited support for several other protocols including TLS/SSL, Internet Gopher, and HTTPS.

The advantages of the Squid proxy server are as follows:

- **Caching**: Caching frequently requested web pages, media files, and other content accelerates response time and reduces bandwidth congestion.
- **Open source**: Squid was originally designed to run as a daemon on Unix-like systems. A Windows port was maintained up to version 2.7. New versions available on Windows use the Cygwin environment. Squid is free software released under the GNU general public license.
- **Efficient**: A Squid proxy server is usually installed on a separate server than the web server with the original files. Squid works by tracking object use over the network. Initially, it acts as an intermediary, simply passing the client's request on to the server and saving a copy of the requested object. If the same client or multiple clients request the same object before it expires from Squid's cache, Squid can then immediately serve it, accelerating the download and saving bandwidth.

- **Tried and tested**: Internet Service Providers, or ISPs, have been using Squid proxy servers since the early 1990s to provide faster download speeds and reduce latency, especially for delivering rich media and streaming video. Website operators frequently use Squid proxy servers as content accelerators. They cache frequently-viewed content and ease the loads on the web servers. Content delivery networks and media companies use Squid proxy servers and deploy them throughout their networks. This improves viewer experience, particularly for load balancing and handling traffic spikes for popular content.

Let's try to understand the Squid proxy server in this example implementation:

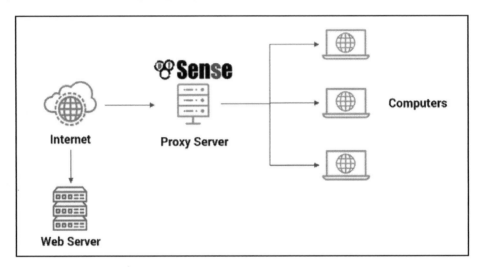

The cloud icon represents the **Internet**. The **Proxy Server** is connected to the **Internet**. This **Proxy Server** is basically pfSense acting as a Squid proxy server. There is also a **Web Server** connected to the **Internet**. And finally, there are computers or users. Traffic can be generated from any of these devices. Squid is a caching proxy for the web. It supports HTTP, FTP, HTTPS, and many other protocols. It also reduces bandwidth and improves the response time by caching and reusing frequently requested web pages. It has extensive access controls and makes a great server accelerator. It runs on almost all available operating systems, including Windows. Hundreds of internet providers worldwide use Squid proxy to provide their users with the best possible web access. It optimizes data flow between the client and the server to improve performance, and caches frequently used content to save bandwidth.

Installing the Squid proxy server

Now let's go ahead and install the Squid proxy server on the pfSense server. Open the pfSense server and use the user credentials to log in. Here on the pfSense dashboard, click **System**, and click **Package Manager**. Click the **Available Packages** tab. pfSense will go out to the public repositories and fetch the list of available packages that you can install on this pfSense instance. Once the list of packages finishes loading, scroll down and search for the squid package. Click the **Install** button. Click the **Confirm** button, and wait for the installation to complete. pfSense will now fetch the installation binaries for this package and install it:

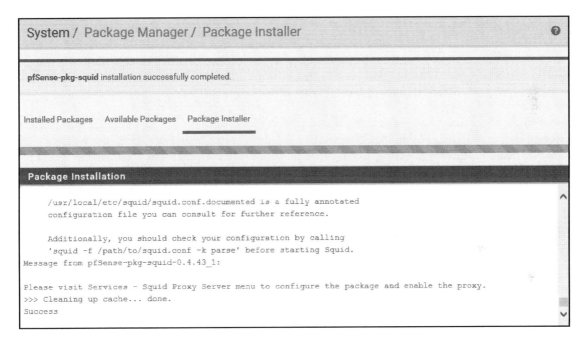

Let's wait for the installation to finish. Now, the Squid package has been installed successfully on this pfSense instance.

Let's review the setup once again to make sure you get a clear picture:

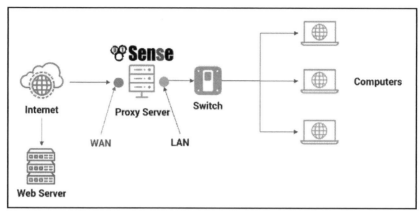

The most important thing to understand here is how the Squid proxy fits between the **WAN** and **LAN** connections in this scenario. This is a typical scenario for setting up your pfSense and Squid proxy server. The **WAN** port is the public interface, which connects your network to the outside world. The Squid proxy and pfSense are installed on the pfSense server. This pfSense server is connected to a local switch, which is part of the internal **LAN** network. So, as is evident from the diagram, this scenario shows that all the endpoints are connected to the **LAN** port through the switch. The port where the internet connection terminates is the **WAN** port. When the client devices within the **LAN** network make requests via the Squid proxy, it will need to manage all that traffic on the **LAN** port. This is an important point to remember. We will need to use this while configuring the Squid proxy server.

Configuring the Squid proxy server

After the installation of Squid is successful, let's go ahead and configure the Squid proxy server. Click **Services**, and select **Squid Proxy Server**. First, you must enable the Squid proxy server:

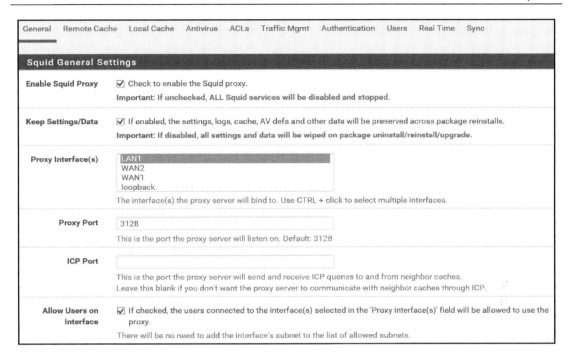

By default, Squid servers are disabled and stopped. Click the **Check to enable the Squid proxy** checkbox. This next setting is to preserve the settings or logs, and so on, across Squid packages installs and reinstalls. It is a good idea to keep this enabled unless you have strong reasons to disable it.

When it comes to proxying a particular interface, the only one you need to pick is the LAN interface. As explained earlier, the LAN user's outgoing requests to the internet only need to go through the proxy. And, the incoming requests from the internet or requests from the DMZ LAN segment may not need to be proxies via Squid. The port is the network port on which this proxy server will listen for incoming connections. The client devices on the network will need to configure this port and the IP address of this pfSense system to connect to the outside world via the Squid proxy server. Let's make sure you check the checkbox for **Allow Users on Interface**. This helps with an easier configuration of your LAN network devices. You can accept default values for the rest of the settings in this section.

Now, let's proceed to the **Transparent Proxy Settings** section:

Transparent Proxy Settings

Transparent HTTP Proxy	☑ Enable transparent mode to forward all requests for destination port 80 to the proxy server. ⓘ Transparent proxy mode works without any additional configuration being necessary on clients. **Important:** Transparent mode will filter SSL (port 443) if you enable 'HTTPS/SSL Interception' below. **Hint:** In order to proxy both HTTP and HTTPS protocols **without intercepting SSL connections**, configure WPAD/PAC options on your DNS/DHCP servers.
Transparent Proxy Interface(s)	LAN1 WAN2 WAN1 The interface(s) the proxy server will transparently intercept requests on. Use CTRL + click to select multiple interfaces.
Bypass Proxy for Private Address Destination	☐ Do not forward traffic to Private Address Space (RFC 1918) destinations. Destinations in Private Address Space (RFC 1918) are passed directly through the firewall, not through the proxy server.
Bypass Proxy for These Source IPs	Do not forward traffic from these **source** IPs, CIDR nets, hostnames, or aliases through the proxy server but let it pass directly through the firewall. **Applies only to transparent mode.** Separate entries by semi-colons (;)
Bypass Proxy for These Destination IPs	Do not proxy traffic going to these **destination** IPs, CIDR nets, hostnames, or aliases, but let it pass directly through the firewall. **Applies only to transparent mode.** Separate entries by semi-colons (;)

Let's also make sure you select the **Enable transparent mode** checkbox. Doing this ensures that you don't have to configure any client environment for proxy settings. This will automatically direct all traffic to the proxy server. Once again, make sure the **Transparent Proxy Interface(s)** is the LAN interface, which is already selected by default. Let's scroll down.

Here's the section on **SSL Man In the Middle Filtering**:

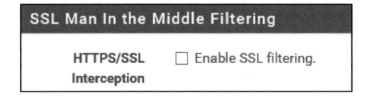

By default, Squid proxy servers cannot monitor encrypted HTTPS traffic. When a client requests a resource over an HTTPS channel, Squid establishes a TCP connection to the destination server on port 443, which is the default port for HTTPs. And, it responds to the client with an HTTP 200 response to indicate the connection was established. Once this encrypted tunnel has been established, Squid passes the packets between the client and the server. But, it no longer has any visibility to the traffic, since it is protected by SSL encryption.

Over the last few years, many popular websites including Google, YouTube, Reddit, and Facebook have started enabling HTTPS encryption by default. This means that without configuring HTTPS interception, Squid proxies have limited filtering, monitoring, and logging capabilities. Fortunately, Squid supports the man-in-the-middle SSL filtering, which will allow you to more effectively monitor the traffic passing through the proxy server. You should certainly consider enabling this option for production environments. But, for the test setup, you can keep things simple and skip this setting.

In the **Logging Settings**, you can also check the **Enable Access Logging** checkbox:

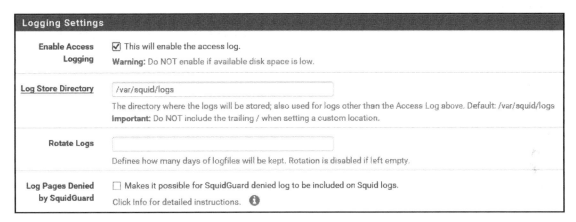

This will configure Squid to log all requests. This may be helpful for auditing and diagnostic purposes. But, be warned that in a busy network, this can produce a lot of logs. And, if you're running low on disk space on your Squid server, this may end up filling up all your hard drive space. So, please plan accordingly before enabling this checkbox. You do have the ability to set the path where you want to save those log files. And, you can enable log rotation to alleviate the problem of a lot of logs piling up on your server. Let's accept the default values for other settings. After configuring the server like so, let's save this configuration.

Before you save the configuration, there is one more setting you should modify. In the **Visible Hostname** under **Headers Handling, Language and Other Customizations**, field, change the default value from **localhost** to `PacktProxy`:

Headers Handling, Language and Other Customizations	
Visible Hostname	PacktProxy This is the hostname to be displayed in proxy server error messages.
Administrator's Email	admin@localhost This is the email address displayed in error messages to the users.
Error Language	en ▾ Select the language in which the proxy server will display error messages to users.
X-Forwarded Header Mode	(on) ▾ Choose how to handle X-Forwarded-For headers. Default: on ⓘ
Disable VIA Header	☐ If not set, Squid will include a Via header in requests and replies as required by RFC2616.

Now scroll down, and click the **Save** button. With that, the basic configuration settings for this Squid proxy server instance are now saved. Now, let's configure the cache for the Squid proxy. Click the **Local Cache** tab.

Scroll down. In the **Do Not Cache** field, you can enter a list of websites or domains that you do not want to cache. These could be sites whose content you want to keep private or secure; for instance, your banking sites, health record sites, and so on. For this demo, you can enter `google.com` and `yahoo.com` on separate lines here:

Do Not Cache	google.com yahoo.com | Enter domain(s) and/or IP address(es) that should never be cached. Put each entry on a separate line.
Enable Offline Mode	☐ Enable this option and the proxy server will never try to validate cached objects. Offline mode gives access to more cached information than normally allowed (e.g., expired cached versions where the origin server should have been contacted otherwise).

And, with this configuration, Squid does not cache any pages or objects from these two domains. Here's another setting called **Enable Offline Mode**. When you enable this option, the proxy server will never try to validate cached objects. Basically, the cached objects may live in cache perpetually. Although this may give you a performance boost, you may end up serving stale content to your users. For that purpose, it is not recommended that you enable this setting.

Now, we come to the most important section, the **Squid Hard Disk Cache Settings**:

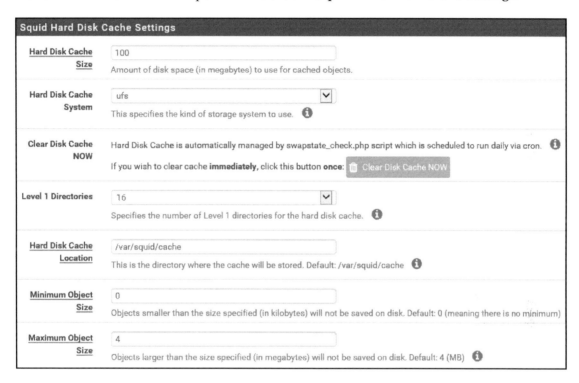

First and foremost, you can set the **Hard Disk Cache Size** here. The default value is 100 MB. If you have a bigger drive and you want to increase the cache size, you can configure that here. If you feel the need to clear the cache, you can click the **Clear Disk Cache NOW** button. You can also set the **Hard Disk Cache Location**. The minimum and maximum sizes of objects that can be saved in the cache are also listed here. These sizes are also in megabytes.

So, the largest object this Squid proxy will cache is 4 MB. Anything bigger than that will not be cached. Next is the **Squid Memory Cache Settings**. Squid has these multiple layers of cache:

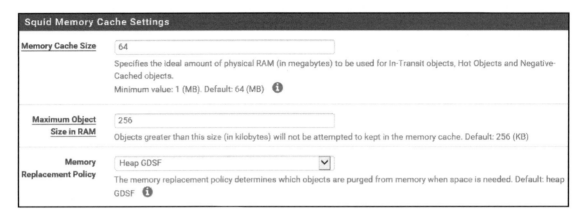

Obviously, the in-memory cache is much faster than the disk-based cache, but you need to be careful when configuring this section. Make sure you don't starve your pfSense server out of all the memory; otherwise, other vital functions of the pfSense server may suffer. Currently, the **Memory Cache Size** is set to **64** MB. This sounds reasonable. The **Maximum Object Size in RAM** is **256** KB, which also seems reasonable. And finally, we come to the section about **Dynamic and Update Content**:

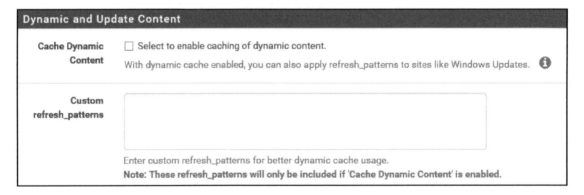

You generally do not want to enable the **Cache Dynamic Content** checkbox, because it will take up too much space in the cache and slow down the server. So, after configuring the pfSense server cache settings, let's click the **Save** button.

The basic configuration is complete. Let's go through the remaining tabs. Switch to **Remote Cache**.

There are no settings here. With **Remote Cache**, you can integrate this Squid proxy server to a remote cache server.

Click the **Antivirus** tab:

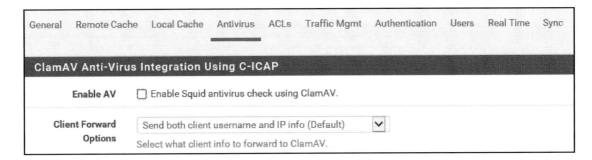

Squid can run an antivirus for all the objects saved in the cache. This is a good security option. You can select the **Enable Squid antivirus check using ClamAV** checkbox to enable an antivirus. The antivirus product used by Squid is called ClamAV. You can also configure a custom URL where the user will be redirected to when Squid detects an infected object:

This is a very handy feature and generally leads to a safer network environment.

You can also choose to leave this as **never**, and manually update the antivirus whenever needed. Click the **Save** button. Now, click the **ACLs** tab:

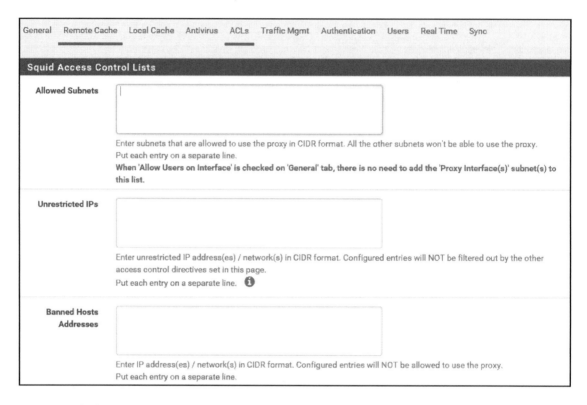

ACL stands for **Access Control List**. You can control users' subnets access levels here. In the **Allowed Subnets** field, type in your required subnets. For example, `192.168.1.0/24`.

Keep in mind that if you have more than one subnet accessing this proxy, you need to specify each subnet on its own line. Please note that the proxy interface subnet is already allowed by default.

There is also a setting for **Unrestricted IPs**. These IPs will bypass the ACL restriction. This may be needed for some system-level nodes running some special processes, or for system administrators who may need unrestricted access to the network. Similarly, **Banned Hosts Addresses** is the opposite of the previous setting. These IPs will not be able to access the proxy server. You have options to **Whitelist** and **Blacklist** certain domains:

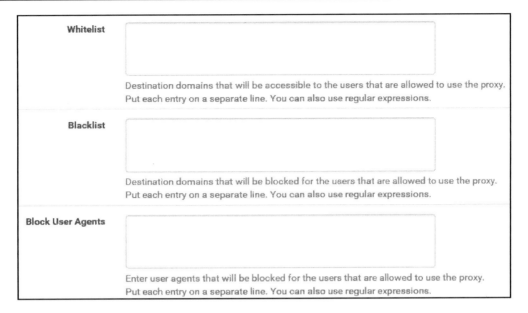

These domains will not be accessible to the proxy users. You can add any unwanted sites here, such as sites containing any offensive materials. In some stricter organizations, social media and news sites can also be banned using this functionality.

Blocked User Agents will restrict the use of specific browsers in your network. Click the **Traffic Mgmt** tab:

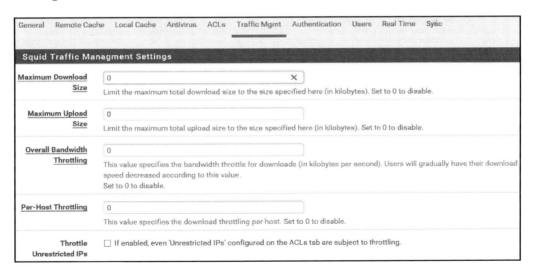

You can set the **Maximum Download Size**, **Maximum Upload Size**, and other similar settings here. There are tons of other settings you can tweak to configure the Squid proxy exactly the way you want. In this example, you went over the most significant settings.

Now that the Squid proxy has been installed and configured on the pfSense server, let's go ahead and observe how the clients can access the internet via this proxy.

Testing the Squid proxy server

Back in the Windows 7 client machine, let's confirm the IP address for this client machine. Launch the Command Prompt window and execute `ipconfig`:

```
C:\Users\packt>ipconfig

Windows IP Configuration

Ethernet adapter Local Area Connection:

   Connection-specific DNS Suffix  . :
   Link-local IPv6 Address . . . . . : fe80::780c:d57c:aef3:2b13%11
   IPv4 Address. . . . . . . . . . . : 192.168.1.2
   Subnet Mask . . . . . . . . . . . : 255.255.255.0
   Default Gateway . . . . . . . . . : fe80::1:1%11
                                       192.168.1.1

Tunnel adapter isatap.{D17026F3-1D71-4EF0-B8F0-E3D4285DCA7B}:

   Media State . . . . . . . . . . . : Media disconnected
   Connection-specific DNS Suffix  . :

C:\Users\packt>_
```

Here, the IP address of this machine is 192.168.1.2. If you check, you will see that this client machine can connect to the internet.

You did not have to make any special configuration for assigning a proxy server to this browser. And, the reason why that is working is because of the setup. The Squid proxy server has been configured as a transparent proxy.

Let's switch to the pfSense webConfigurator in the **ACLs** section for the Squid proxy server. When you scroll down, you find the option called **Banned Hosts Addresses**. As discussed earlier, if you add an IP address to this list, Squid proxy will actively reject the requests from that IP address. Effectively, the banned IP addresses or the networks in CIDR format will be banned from accessing the internet. Let's enter the IP address of the Windows 7 client machine here, and observe the effects. Let's enter 192.168.1.2:

And, click the **Save** button. Now, the client machine's IP address has been banned.

Let's switch to that client machine and try to access the internet again. Refresh the browser, and you will see the browser is not able to get any response back.

The Squid proxy server denied the request, and the user got this message: The requested URL could not be retrieved.

So, this is how you can ban certain IP addresses from accessing the internet. The message also provides the email address of the Squid proxy administrator. This is helpful for the end users to be able to contact the network support and resolve any issues. The email address admin@localhost is the default email address configured by the Squid proxy.

Let's see how you can change this to a proper email address.

Switch back to the pfSense webConfigurator. In the Squid proxy management page, switch to the **General** tab. Scroll down to find a setting called **Administrator's Email**. This is where you can set the value for the correct email address. Let's change the administrator's email to packtpub.n@outlook.com:

Click **Save**.

Now, let's switch to the Windows 7 client machine, and refresh the web page. You will see that the user still gets the Access Denied error page, but this time the proxy server's administrator email address is showing the correct value. Now, let's revert the changes you made to the banned IP address list. Switch to the ACLs tab. Delete this IP address from **Banned Hosts Addresses**. And, click **Save**.

If you refresh the browser on the client machine, you will see that it can access the internet once again. That was the functionality to ban specific IP addresses.

Now, let's try out another functionality to restrict access. This is called **Blacklist**:

Blacklist	google.com
	Destination domains that will be blocked for the users that are allowed to use the proxy. Put each entry on a separate line. You can also use regular expressions.

Here, you can blacklist certain domains for your entire user base. Let's say you, for some insane reason, want to blacklist google.com. You can add that domain here. Click **Save**. Notice that the specific client IP address is no longer banned. Now, on the client web browser, try to refresh the page which is trying to access google.com. And notice again, the user will get the Access Denied page error. This is how you can ban certain domains.

Let's go back and remove google.com from the blacklist and click **Save**. Now, we're back to the original settings.

So, so far you've learned that there are many ways within the Squid proxy management to restrict the IP addresses or certain domains. But, that is just scratching the surface. Squid is capable of much more than that.

You can also restrict download sizes under the **Traffic Management** tab. Before changing any of those settings, let's go ahead and try to download a large file. So, you want to download the full installer of .Net Framework from Microsoft's site. Let's switch to the Windows 7 client machine, and launch the web browser. Search for *download microsoft dot net framework version 4.0*. And, try to download it. When you get the option to download, click **Save**. The file starts to download without any problems.

You will notice the speed of the download is pretty fast. Let's cancel the download. And, let's go back to the pfSense web GUI. Now, let's switch to the **Traffic Management** tab. Let's set the **Per-Host Throttling** to the value of 10:

Per-Host Throttling	10 ✕
	This value specifies the download throttling per host. Set to 0 to disable.

This will limit the bandwidth allocated to each client. **Per-Host Throttling** sets the maximum amount of bandwidth an individual host can use. In this case, it will limit the bandwidth to 10 KB per second. Let's save this configuration and switch to the Windows 7 client machine, and try to download the .Net Framework installer file again.

You will notice that the time to download the file has increased greatly as compared to the previous download time. This is because pfSense is limiting the bandwidth allocated to any single host or device on the network. So, this is how you can leverage all the features provided by Squid and pfSense to control and shape your traffic exactly the way you like.

Summary

In this chapter, you learned all about proxy servers, what they are, and their key features. You also gained an understanding of the advantages of a Squid proxy server. Next, you learned how to install and configure a Squid proxy server. And finally, you learned how to test the Squid proxy server in a client environment. And with that, we come to the end of our book on managing network security with the pfSense firewall.

In this book, you got an in-depth look at the pfSense firewall, its inner workings, and how you can use it to manage your network security and access. You started off with an introduction to pfSense, where you gained an understanding of what pfSense is, its key features, and advantages. You also went through a series of demonstrations on the installation of pfSense on a virtual server. Next, you learned how to configure pfSense as a firewall. You also learned how to create and manage multiple firewall rules. Then, you configured pfSense for failover and load balancing. After that, you learned all about IPsec, its features, and how it is used. And, you also learned how to configure an IPsec VPN tunnel in a pfSense server. Finally, you learned how to configure pfSense as a Squid proxy server. You integrated the Squid proxy into pfSense, and then tested it using client access.

Other Books You May Enjoy

If you enjoyed this book, you may be interested in these other books by Packt:

Mastering pfSense - Second Edition

David Zientara

ISBN: 978-1-78899-317-3

- Configure pfSense services such as DHCP, Dynamic DNS, captive portal, DNS, NTP and SNMP
- Set up a managed switch to work with VLANs
- Use pfSense to allow, block and deny traffic, and to implement Network Address Translation (NAT)
- Make use of the traffic shaper to lower and raise the priority of certain types of traffic
- Set up and connect to a VPN tunnel with pfSense
- Incorporate redundancy and high availability by utilizing load balancing and the Common Address Redundancy Protocol (CARP)
- Explore diagnostic tools in pfSense to solve network problems

Mastering Linux Security and Hardening
Donald A. Tevault

ISBN: 978-1-78862-030-7

- Use various techniques to prevent intruders from accessing sensitive data
- Prevent intruders from planting malware, and detect whether malware has been planted
- Prevent insiders from accessing data that they aren't authorized to access
- Do quick checks to see whether a computer is running network services that it doesn't need to run
- Learn security techniques that are common to all Linux distros, and some that are distro-specific

Leave a review - let other readers know what you think

Please share your thoughts on this book with others by leaving a review on the site that you bought it from. If you purchased the book from Amazon, please leave us an honest review on this book's Amazon page. This is vital so that other potential readers can see and use your unbiased opinion to make purchasing decisions, we can understand what our customers think about our products, and our authors can see your feedback on the title that they have worked with Packt to create. It will only take a few minutes of your time, but is valuable to other potential customers, our authors, and Packt. Thank you!

Index

A

Access Control List (ACL) 132
active-active load balancing 86
active-passive failover 85

C

Certificate Revocation Lists (CRLs) 38

D

De-Militarized Zone (DMZ) 59
DHCP server
  pfSense, configuring 45, 46, 48, 49, 50, 51, 52, 53, 55, 56

F

failover
  about 84, 85, 86, 87
  across multiple WAN connections 88, 89
  verifying, across multiple WAN connections 97, 98, 99
firewall rules
  creating, in pfSense 72, 74, 75
  for internal LAN network 76, 77, 78
  managing 81
  setting up 65, 66, 67, 68, 70
  setting up, for LAN2 78, 79, 80, 81
firewall
  about 57, 58, 60
  pfSense, configuring 60, 62, 64, 65
FreeBSD 6
Fully Qualified Domain Name (FQDN) 30

G

Gateway Groups
  configuring 90, 91, 93, 94, 95

I

internal LAN network
  firewall rules, setting up 76, 77, 78
Internet Protocol Security (IPsec)
  about 101
  features 103
  transport mode 102
  tunnel mode 102
IPSec VPN tunnel
  configuring 105, 106, 107, 108, 109, 110, 111, 112, 113
  implementation 104
  phases 105
  prerequisites 105

L

load balancing
  about 83, 85, 86, 87
  across multiple WAN connections 88, 89
  verifying, across multiple WAN connections 96, 97

M

m0n0wall project 6
multiple WAN connections
  failover 88, 89
  failover, verifying 97, 98, 99
  load balancing 88, 89
  load balancing, verifying 96, 97

N

Network Address Translation (NAT) 10

P

pfSense firewall rules

configuring 113, 114, 115, 116
pfSense WebGUI
  exploring 36, 38, 39, 40, 42, 43, 44
pfSense, use cases
  DHCP or DNS server 10
  firewall 9
  LAN or WAN router 9
  multi-WAN router support, for failover 10
  multi-WAN router support, for load balancer 10
  Network Address Translation (NAT) 10
  port forwarding 10
  VPN router 9
  wireless hotspot or captive portal 9
pfSense
  about 6
  benefits 8
  configuring 25, 26, 27, 29, 30, 31, 32, 33, 34, 35
  configuring, as DHCP server 45, 46, 48, 49, 50, 51, 52, 53, 55, 56
  configuring, as firewall 60, 62, 64, 65
  features 7, 11, 12
  firewall rules, creating 72, 74, 75
  installation, completing 19, 20, 21, 22, 25
  installing 6
  installing, on virtual machine 15, 16, 17

pre-requisites 12, 13, 14
reference 8, 12, 15
Pre-Shared Key (PSK) 107
proxy server
  about 120
  Squid proxy server 121, 122

S

Security Association (SA) 103
Squid proxy server
  about 121
  advantages 121
  configuring 124, 125, 126, 127, 128, 129, 130, 132, 133, 134
  installing 123, 124
  testing 134, 135, 136

V

virtual machine
  configuring 19, 20, 21, 22, 24
  launching 18, 19
  pfSense, installing 15, 16, 17

W

Web-based Graphical User Interface (WebGUI) 33

Made in the USA
San Bernardino, CA
20 July 2019